Esprit de corps

Leadership for progressive change in local government

Barry Quirk

The **Joseph Rowntree Foundation** has supported this project as part of its programme of research and innovative development projects, which it hopes will be of value to policy makers, practitioners and service users. The facts presented and views expressed in this report are, however, those of the author and not necessarily those of the Foundation.

Barry Quirk is the Chief Executive of the London Borough of Lewisham and Visiting Fellow of Social Policy and Politics at Goldsmiths College. This paper is written in a personal capacity. In order not to disrupt the text, references to source documents have been kept to a minimum. A full list of references and further reading is given under chapter headings at the end of the paper.

Published for the Joseph Rowntree Foundation by YPS

ISBN 1 84263 030 X

Cover design by Adkins Design

Prepared and printed by:
York Publishing Services Ltd
64 Hallfield Road
Layerthorpe
York
YO31 7ZQ
Tel: 01904 430033 Fax: 01904 430868 E-mail: orders@yps.ymn.co.uk

CONTENTS

COMMENTARY

How extraordinary it is that Britain's biggest business is so little understood and so much looked down upon by those who make their living elsewhere in the economy.

Which captains of industry see local government as an excellent training ground from which to recruit able managers and deep professionals? How many Whitehall mandarins naturally seek advice from local government officers about the best way to get things done on the ground? Yet local government has to cope with a level of complexity and ambiguity – generated by the range and depth of its activities, by political direction, by its funding, by the variety and inescapability of its customers – which would leave most other organisations gasping.

Of course local government shoots itself brilliantly in the foot by failing to manage its reputation, so that the person in the street sees it as at best worthy and boring, and at worst – judged by the antics of a handful of authorities – incompetent and corrupt. Local government has always seemed to me blind about the importance of external and internal communication, as if it was an indulgence rather than essential to the success of any large enterprise. This is not helped by confusion about what local government is for. It is remarkable that central government can carry out, successively over the years, huge exercises about local government's financing, structure and political direction without first nailing down what it expects local government to be do. How easily we misunderstand the importance of local government in holding together the fabric – in every sense of that word – of our society.

Is it good or bad that different authorities have different priorities and standards and spend their money in different ways? What should be the relationship of local authorities to schools? To the police? To the NHS? Indeed, to central government? Is local government just a delivery vehicle for central government programmes? How much freedom should local government have to raise and spend its money as it sees fit? Why does every incoming central government, whatever its colour, promise local government more discretion and end up reducing it?

Not all is gloom. The coming together of the divided representative bodies into the single Local Government Association and the creation of the Improvement and Development Agency are a major step in giving local government one voice and a focus on constructive change through peer support. The Liverpools are being turned round. There are signs that the necessary but insufficient focus on managerialism (performance indicators, efficiency projects and so forth) is broadening to a much greater interest in local government's ability to catalyse and encourage action by others in the locality. The concept of the mayor and cabinet, most vividly of course in London, creates the opportunity to give stronger leadership and to attract more able people to local government service.

The genuine understanding that a local authority is not a set of departments (not infrequently at war with one another) but is there to serves groups of users is being turned into practicality, for example in Hertfordshire where the former social services and education departments were united in April 2001 to create a single service with a new ethos focused on children, schools and families. Most importantly of all, this attention to the user is growing into a renewed and very welcome interest in local government's role in building a greater sense of community.

Against this background, Barry Quirk offers a fresh look at what is required to carry local government to the next stage of development. He sets out 'a ten point blueprint', ranging from getting the basics right in order to earn credibility through to more imaginative ways of engaging with citizens. But 'need to' lists, whatever the merits of the items on them, invite the retort, 'yes, this may well be right, but what is going to make it happen?' They are like my doctor's advice that I 'need to' lose weight, drink less, exercise more … all that I know: how do I find the energy and willpower to do it? Refreshingly, the interest of this document is less in the mechanics than in the spirit of a local authority, and therein lies the answer.

Alongside organisation design which addresses the corrosive 'guild professionalism' of local government and the building of managerial and organisational competence, Quirk emphasises the leadership needed to create high energy, high self-esteem, outward-looking authorities to which able people are proud to belong. Surely if there is a starting-place for change it is in raising the standard of leaders, upper and lower case 'l', in local government. It is no coincidence that in the private sector, as the world spins faster and the future is harder to descry, the importance of leadership – at all levels, as Quirk says – comes to the fore. My own firm has had more enquiries about leadership development and its link to emotional commitment and organisational change than any other topic in the last year.

To an external eye, local government offers both the highs and lows of organisational behaviour. Highs like the young woman spending her evenings in a damp underpass on a bleak 60s housing estate with fifteen year old girls who are not welcome at home, talking about their hopes and making them feel better about themselves – and doing so for an annual salary many City workers would sneer at per month. Lows like the assistant director pointing to a table two feet deep in paper received from government departments in the last few weeks and saying he hopes the thirteenth draft of a document he is working on for a committee will be accepted. Highs like the authority which freed a junior team to find a better way of statementing children with special educational needs who then figured out how to do it in half the time at less cost. Lows like the chief executive droning about 'partnership development strategies' while I could see through his office window an overspilling skip of rotting garbage in the council car park which I knew had been there six months.

The airport bookstalls groan with tomes about commercial management, for which there is clearly a huge market. Why, when the performance of the public sector is so importance to all of us as citizens, is there no equivalent literature about its management? Barry Quirk contributes to the long task of narrowing the gap. We live in an era when the sense of community in Britain, of having a duty to my neighbours and to the environment around me, is perhaps at an all time low. How right he is to call for building *esprit de corps* amongst politicians, managers and staff, and through that amongst the public they serve – and how important it is that we hear his call.

Stephen Taylor
April 2001

Note
Stephen Taylor is a non-executive director of the Improvement and Development Agency and a director of the consulting firm Stanton Marris. The views expressed here are his own.

FOREWORD

There can be no doubt about the challenges now facing local government. As a result of worldwide pressures, we work in an era of highly mobile capital, accelerating communication and aggressive individualism. The agenda is common across national boundaries and by no means confined to the local level. We face questions about the very future of representative democracy; growing concern for social cohesion; challenges to established public sector values and practices; and a common drive to secure ever better value in public expenditure. It is a heady mix for anyone attempting to explore a way forward.

Barry Quirk's stimulating paper reflects his practical approach and represents a valuable contribution to the current debate. Barry does not talk loosely of cultural change as if it were the equivalent of a new 'paint-job' or of transformation as if it were practised by hairdressers. Instead, he emphasises the importance of local leadership in 'building a sense of place and belonging', and firmly links that leadership with a 'disciplined approach' to designing and delivering services.

Barry reminds us that, whilst service provision is not a right of local government, it does confer substantial authority and muscle to local governance if done well. His agenda stresses the importance of basic services and, as we stand on the edge of a change that will introduce executive politicians, he rightly underlines the significance of a strong partnership between political and managerial leadership founded on clear expectations, accountabilities and complementary efforts. His approach concentrates on progressive change underpinned by sound performance management: clear objectives, sharp responsibilities, effective monitoring and recognition of progress. He rightly endorses a non-ideological approach to securing service provision and warns us of the dangers of getting lost in unfocused process.

Barry's conclusion that 'spirited communities need spirited Councils' and that this calls for the development of an *esprit de corps* amongst politicians, managers and employees is welcome. He offers a comprehensive common-sense manifesto for change, which will appeal to many. Let's bring out the tambourines and get on with the job – no one else can rise to this challenge at the local level.

Sir Michael Lyons
Chief Executive
Birmingham City Council

1 INTRODUCTION

In the current age, distant events occurring across the globe have an impact on our everyday lives in ways that did not happen in the past. Information and communication technologies are enveloping the globe in the first decade of this century just as electricity did in the first decade of the last century. Furthermore, the rise of computer-mediated entertainment encourages the global spread of cultural connections. Just over 100 years ago, transportation costs began to reduce significantly so as to increase the mobility of people. We now find that the collapsing costs of telecommunication serves to create a globalised world of information where the time distance for communication between any two people anywhere in the world is just one-eighth of one second. We witness not just the increased mobility of people but also the vastly increased mobility of their knowledge.

But these trends have not led, for the majority of people, to the death of distance or the loss of locality. Closer events still have the biggest influence upon us. And, for each of us, local, locale and locality still matter more than global and universal. We can converse across the globe but we occupy space and place somewhere: in some geographically unique and distinctive locality. It may be inner urban, suburban or rural in character and it may be ever more connected to and dependent upon other (regional, national and global) economies. But it is local nonetheless.

And yet, despite the fact that local events continue to have a predominant influence upon us, the institution of local government is the forgotten relative in so many conversations about Government and the public sector. Political and media attention centres on the debate about how best to improve the performance of schools and hospitals. These are local institutions and yet they seem to have gained a national character somehow devoid of local content. They are depicted in the media as though they are aspatial 'frontlines' of public services with funding streams direct from the Minister's office. Debates about the quality of schools and hospitals are vital. But they do not describe the totality of the issues facing local public services.

This point is also seen at moments of crisis. In the heat of the fuel distribution crisis in September 2000, it was the health service that was placed on 'red alert' by Ministers. There is no doubt; the emergency in health was very real. And, yet, most of local government had just a couple of days' left of fuel, was in real danger of systemic failure but received barely a mention in the public debate. This was a little odd given that it was the image of uncollected rubbish in the streets and the stories of Council workers not burying the dead that were to characterise the 1979 'winter of discontent' and presage the end of the Callaghan Labour Government. Local government seems to have disappeared from the national debate or at least to have a very low profile.

This paper is a small attempt to begin to redress this imbalance. Local government is at the frontline of change in the public sector. Local government secures services that matter – services that set the context for people to experience a good quality of life and improved quality of life-chances. Local government has the capacity to foster enterprise and confidence in localities as well as to promote civic virtue, pride and social harmony. But it can only realise this wider capacity if it is relevant, progressive and effective. There is no single route for Councils to follow: success rarely follows formulae. But, for communities to thrive, their

Councils need to do more than just survive current pressures. They need to transcend them. And to do that they need effective local leadership.

Just as every government has many citizens, so each citizen has several governments. As individuals, we each elect some six or seven politicians to represent our interests in the various tiers of government that choose between competing views of the common good at differing geographical scales. We choose others to choose on our behalf. And the evidence is that, while we increasingly acclaim democratic processes as the best to settle choices, we also increasingly mistrust the democratic institutions that we elect to make these choices. This is not a comment narrowly focused on British local government. It applies with uncomfortable force across the world's developed democracies. Public concern, once focused upon market failure, is now just as likely to be focused on government failure – failure of democracies to secure public services that are valued by citizens and failure of democratic institutions to connect with fast-paced changes in daily life and wider civil society.

In very many ways, the government that is closest to the citizen is also the most local. Just as experience of public service is mostly local, so too is experience as a citizen. That's why local government matters. It is the basis for public provision and action, as well as the starting point for civic engagement. Hence, this paper starts from the premise that local government should be effective, should be progressive and should actively engage its citizens.

The argument is not that local government needs to be bigger nor needs substantially more powers or resources. More powers and additional resources might resolve some issues but of themselves they will not turn ineffective Councils around. No, the argument here is that Councils need more effective political and managerial leadership. And it is not just leadership at the top that is needed but 'deep leadership' through all levels. At its simplest, leadership, in local government, differs from management in that it goes beyond 'doing a job well' and takes wider responsibility for making a positive difference within local communities. A central aspect of this paper will be to examine modern approaches to leadership for public purpose: leadership for the institution of local government and leadership for the wider community.

In a world awash with complex and fast-paced changes, people need attachments, belonging and purpose as well as effective public services. Yes, people want a sense that their Council is developing more relevant and better services, but they also want them to develop a more supportive community and a shared sense of place. For the majority, their local community is the best place to discover shared meaning and mutual action with others.

Those politicians and commentators who wish for progressive change in local government focus on the financial and other incentives. This paper will refer to these debates but the overarching stress, here, is on how to develop intrinsic motivation rather than extrinsic incentives.

Councils are not engaged on a process of change for its own sake. They exist to improve life in their localities. In short, they seek a progressive change in the fortunes of people living in specific 'places'. They seek one purpose: 'improving life for people in this local area'.

This requires them to accentuate the distinctive character of their localities and build on the comparative advantage of the places they represent. English local government is composed of some 130 'upper-tier' authorities with social services and education functions. Approximately one-half of these are Unitary

Councils in urban or metropolitan areas (33 in London alone) and one-half are composed of County Councils. The remaining 270 or so Councils are smaller District Councils representing a range of different areas from outlying and sparsely populated rural areas to fairly large towns. This is the variety and diversity of English local government.

The widespread policy of regenerating communities (that began in the early 1990s) by a mixed development of people and place is correct. But community renewal does not work if it is not grounded in local circumstance. It needs to start from the distinctive character of a locality: from its strengths and latent opportunities. There are many examples within local government of Councils fostering economic competitiveness in their areas by leveraging external investment into them. But there are too few examples where Councils have built on their uniqueness by encouraging the development of specific economic clusters (thereby establishing nodes or magnets built on agglomeration economies).

The renewal of place and locality is a central purpose for local government although not a prime concern here. The focus in this paper is on how Councils can become progressive forces for change more generally. The argument here is that by changing themselves they will be more able to act as a catalyst for progressive change in the place and locality they represent.

In this context, the key questions become: how can Councils best develop their leadership; and how can progressive change for community benefit best be assured? Change is needed both to secure better services and in respect of Councils' wider governance and community role. In examining the responsibilities of leadership in progressive change in service delivery; in politics and governance; and, finally, in supportive management arrangements, a range of disciplines will be drawn upon. Public policy analysis, organisational and management theory, political science and psychology each offer useful insights in the narrative that follows. The aim is to outline some key points for politicians, community leaders and managers in local government so as to improve the prospect for more effective local leadership. The paper concludes with a ten-point plan for corporate progressive change.

However, any conclusions about what needs to be done ought to be posited on a thorough appreciation of the actual challenges faced. To decide how progressive change can best be delivered, it is vital first to have a clear understanding of the key concepts of change, progress and leadership as well as an appreciation of the current Government's agenda for change.

2 THE CHARACTER OF CHANGE AND PROGRESS

The character of change is described through metaphor in much of the literature in mathematical terms as linear or non-linear, or in terms of 'natural cycles'. In many ways, the best metaphor for our experience of change is 'change as fire'. Fires consume things; they don't just alter them. Things once burnt can never be unburnt. Fires are all process and no apparent substance. Furthermore, fires change the state of things in quite unpredictable ways. Is this not the essence of change as it is experienced: change as irreversible force and with no clear pre-figured end-state?

But the fire metaphor, while evocatively descriptive, may not be helpful to leaders if they wish to encourage purposive action. For metaphors convey powerful notions as to whether change occurs through external environmental events or through the effects of human agency. And the problem with the fire metaphor is that it implies passivity at worst or unmanageability at best. We need a clearer language to describe change.

Current debates about change carry considerable intellectual baggage from theoretical arguments within both the sciences and the humanities. Within the sciences, the debate centres on which precise blend of random variation, probability and chaos characterises change in the natural world. And, in the humanities, the very notion of human progress is long contested (can there be said to be progress in art?).

The word 'progress' has a complex history in the English language. Its early uses were in respect of physical marches or journeys and contained no ideological content. With the developing notions of 'civilisation' and 'history' in the eighteenth century, the word became associated with advancement. And, since the time of the Enlightenment, it has become received wisdom that improvement is now permanently with us, and that increasing knowledge, technological change and social development are leading inevitably to progress in human affairs.

In Britain, the debate about progress was at its height in the mid-Victorian age with the growing acceptance of the Darwinian paradigm. However, it would be wrong to assume that the words 'progress' and 'evolution' were ever synonyms. The term 'evolution' entered the English language contentiously. It was popularised by Herbert Spencer to infer progress in human development. Darwin long resisted using the word because it implied progressivism in biological development. He wrote, 'after a long reflection, I cannot avoid the conviction that no innate tendency to progressive development exists.' In the past decade, Stephen Jay Gould most powerfully put the current case against progressivism in biology when he argued, 'the vaunted progress of life is really random motion away from simple beginnings, not directed impetus toward inherently advantageous complexity' (Gould, 1996). And thus, while we may often alight upon evolutionary metaphors, any natural or biological inferences about progress remain far from unproblematic.

The parallel debate about progress in human affairs has, however, become a little more one-sided. In the mid-eighteenth century, Edward Young declared, 'nature revolves, but man advances'. Since then, it has become almost universally accepted that scientific and technical developments allied with mass information transmission across the generations are the engine of betterment, advancement and progress. Moreover, it is usually assumed that this progress is inexorable and inevitable. And, in consequence, the prevailing paradigm in politics and social affairs for the past 100 years has been the widespread notion of purposive change for progress.

But, despite the dominance of this mindset, it remains vital to understand that random variation, observed in the natural sciences, characterises a great deal in human affairs. Furthermore, the limits to rational foresight limit our ability to achieve progress without perverse, sour or unintended consequences. No matter how much we wish to, we simply cannot control the future. In many ways, each generation struggles to solve the problems created by its parents. In the book, *The Crooked Timber of Humanity*, Isaiah Berlin expressed it as follows:

> It is true that some problems can be solved, some ills cured, in both individual and social life ... but any study of society shows that every solution creates a new situation which breeds its own new needs and problems, new demands. The children have obtained what their parents and grandparents longed for – greater freedom, greater material welfare, a juster society: but the old ills are forgotten, and the children face new problems, brought about by the very solution of the old ones, and these even if they can in turn be solved, generate new situations, and with them new requirements – and so on – for ever and unpredictably.
>
> (Berlin, 1990)

Berlin's reference is not a cry against progress, rather a mature recognition of progress as an iterative problem-solving process across the generations. What is more, a critical understanding of progress in society generally is different from an understanding of progress at the level of the institution or the individual. Here, relative success and failure tend to be judged against norms at a given point in time.

Progress or success for institutions or individuals is viewed with the benefit of hindsight. And here, as elsewhere, the bias of observational selection bedevils our rationality. An example may help illustrate this point. In the 1940s, the Italian physicist, Enrico Fermi, went to work on the Manhattan Project in the USA (Sagan, 1997). When he arrived, he was introduced to a General and told that he was their greatest battlefield General. Fermi thought about this and asked, 'what makes a great General?' After some discussion they concluded that winning five battles in war was a robust enough criterion. 'Well', said Fermi, 'if armies are equally matched, the chances of winning one battle is 1 in 2; the chance of winning five battles is 1 in 32. How many Generals do you have?' Now, there are nearly 2,700 Generals in the US army and so, according to Fermi, about 90 should have won five battles just by chance! Perhaps, if 120 had won five or more battles, about 30 of these would be great Generals. This tale is a sobering reminder that success is described in retrospect and the patterns of success we map today can often be the workings of random chance rather than the planned and intended actions of those who appear to have succeeded.

The same argument applies more generally to purposive changes in service policy and/or practice. In respect of, say, service innovations, it is likely that the majority of planned changes will either make no difference to service results or worsen service outcomes. Moreover, of those results that are positive, it is probable that a significant share of these would arise by chance; hence, the importance of honest and rapid learning (of a critical and sceptical nature) within organisations.

Within the realm of politics, the term 'progress' has been adopted by political parties of all hues and consequently is used more in the persuasive than in the descriptive sense. It is, however, a term more usually adopted by parties of the Left (sometimes to distinguish between different elements within Left politics), although it has also been adopted by parties of the Centre-Left, Centre and sometimes of the Right.

The call in this paper for progressive change in local government is not an aligned political claim. Nor is it a naive claim to once-and-for-all social improvement. Instead, it is an acceptance that progressive change needs to be purposely lead not simply observed. Leading change progressively requires a mature appreciation of the contextual uncertainties, unpredictabilities and risks. It requires an ability to learn critically and quickly. Moreover, it requires the development of a social or civic entrepreneurship: harnessing underused resources, identifying opportunities and knowing when to be innovative. In local government, progressive leadership is crucial not just for the success of the institution but also to deliver social improvement in local communities.

This is perhaps the central issue for leadership in the current age. At a time when the risks of war appear contained, so we witness the rise of manufactured risks. These either take the form of 'unnatural hazards' that stem from pollution, global warming and new agricultural and industrial processes, or the 'moral hazards' to children and women within their own families and communities. Just as fate was supposed to be conquered and people accepting of a progressive agenda, so risks from persons known and unknown seem now to combine with hazards created by the unintended consequences of our collective efforts to make people feel victims again.

Leadership that will fail is either that which encourages feckless fatalism or that which promulgates reckless certainties. In the twenty-first century, as before, the role of leadership (in local government as much as in wider society) is to help people see how their own purposeful actions can create the prospect of real progress.

3 THE CHANGING CHARACTER OF LEADERSHIP

The hero school of leadership is best left to comic books. So, too, is the narrow approach to 'brigading resources' and commanding actions. Organisations are socially constructed; they are places of emotion as well as rationality, for they are composed of people. And, so, leadership is a difficult art. It requires a lot from those in leading positions.

Within local government, managerial and political leadership are different in character and need to be viewed as complementary in nature. Political leadership derives its credibility from the democratic process; whereas managerial leadership derives its credibility from its merit-based means of appointment. Both retain and sustain their credibility through behaviour and conduct, not through their words.

Unlike managerial authority that stems from knowledge, experience and hierarchy, political authority stems from the legitimacy of election and an expectation that those exercising it are principally concerned with the common good. Citizens only care how much politicians know when they know how much they care.

When the Government's People's Panel were asked what qualities they considered to be most important in a public leader, honesty and trustworthiness easily came top (38 and 37 per cent respectively). Some way behind came being a 'good communicator' and 'competence' (with 26 and 24 per cent respectively) (Cabinet Office, 2000a).

As with public leadership, so, too, with organisational leadership. The overall performance of an organisation can be said to reflect its cultural climate. Moreover, its climate can be said to stem from the style and tone set by an organisation's leaders (particularly the behaviour of leaders in moments of organisational tension or crisis). Thus, the quality of an organisation's leadership is pivotal to its success. The attributes of successful leaders are:

- they establish an overarching vision; they support people to do their best; and they thank them for their efforts

- they have high personal visibility in their organisations; they encourage 'followership'; and they accept a deep accountability for the actions of others

- they challenge established processes; they inspire a shared vision; they enable others to act; and they model the way forward

- they build an appetite for achievement and a spirit of contribution.

Research into leadership effectiveness (Goleman, 2000) shows that leaders who achieve results have a flexible personal style. They can adapt their style according to the specifics of an organisation's environmental circumstances. This means that successful leaders must have a suite of styles that they use according to circumstance. Table 1 shows six different styles and an assessment, all other things being equal, of the relative effectiveness of each style.

Table 1 Six different styles of leadership and the relative effectiveness of each style

Style	Characteristic phrase	Impact
Coercive	'Do what I tell you'	–
Pacesetting	'Do as I do, now'	–
Affiliative	'People come first'	+
Democratic	'What do you think?'	+
Coaching	'Try this'	+
Authoritative	'Come with me'	++

Effective leaders can be said to be those skilled in moderating to circumstance and situation: to audience and to followers. But successful leaders are not unprincipled, moving with the changing winds of circumstance. They moderate, yes; but they also exude integrity and constancy of values and principles. Traditionally in local government, leadership amongst officers stemmed from professionalism, from expertise. This is fast changing. Managerial leadership needs to be appreciative of professional concerns but above all focused on the whole organisation's needs.

Community leadership, however, requires local politicians to engage with everyone. This is, in many ways, much more demanding than managerial leadership as the constituency is not narrow (employees or organisational stakeholders) but universal. It means that councillors need a wide 'register' of communication skills. This is a new feature. Traditionally, political skills are honed in party group meetings or in debating in Council chambers. In this traditional context, effective political skills involved a narrow persuasive range (other politicians in the same party group). These narrow party settings are arenas of less and less relevance in debating and deciding public interest issues.

The political skills that will increasingly count are those that are effective with the media and across a much wider range of public settings. Directly elected mayors will need most of all to develop these skills. And these are extremely difficult skills to acquire and develop. Therefore, it is important that the expectation on councillors is properly expressed, that they are thoroughly supported in their role and that they have development opportunities for sharpening their own leadership.

Furthermore, the development of governance at the local level, the creation of service-based, regeneration-focused or problem-centred partnerships, is demanding new styles of leadership. Leading one institution is different from leading across organisations or in partnership settings. Increasingly, leading politicians and senior managers in local government have to exercise leadership across institutions in respect of health improvement, economic regeneration and community safety partnerships. And the new requirement for Councils to establish cross-sectoral, multi-agency local strategic partnerships further ratchets the demands on local leadership skills.

But, before this paper can examine what local leadership is for and how it can best be conducted, it is crucial to set the demands on local leadership within the context of the Government's wider agenda for change.

4 THE GOVERNMENT'S AGENDA FOR CHANGE

Citizens have expectations of public services that are unfulfilled. The Government's People's Panel assessment of attitudes to public services (Figure 1) shows that the satisfaction levels are lower for Council services than for most other public services.

When the Panel was asked about those Council services with which it was most dissatisfied, housing services scored worst with some 30 per cent, youth services second worst with 25 per cent and most other services received scores of around 10 per cent. And, while it is possible to contest this finding through the

Figure 1 The Government's People's Panel assessment of attitudes to public services

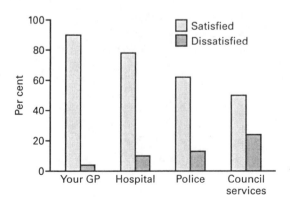

Source: Cabinet Office (2000a).

use of different satisfaction ratings and different techniques, the overall message to local government makes sober reading. Compared to most of the public sector, local government services do not appear to be held in high esteem by the public.

Modernising government and public services is central to political debate. Political parties try to develop their own distinctive stance towards both the substance and style of public sector reform. Together with taxation policy, public sector reform is the centre-piece of political parties' manifestos to govern. Support is won or lost on the credibility of proposed reforms. Hence, the prevailing agenda for change is, and probably always will be, central to the public contest for power.

The legacy of previous Conservative Governments can be described as decentralised service contracting and, more generally, quasi-market approaches. Generally, public institutions (such as schools and hospitals) were encouraged to compete for public service users: either on the basis of the quality of service offered or in enforced competition with the private sector. These quasi-market approaches could have developed further (through vouchers and the like), but they were halted in 1997 when the New Labour Government began to develop more plan-based approaches to change. The most notable break with the past could be seen in the health service where General Practice fund holding and commissioner–provider separation was overtaken by a wholesale reconfiguration of the health sector driven from the centre.

The incoming Government had the twin objectives of devolution in government and substantive improvements in public services. The vital but fragile settlement in Northern Ireland and the differential devolution of powers and functions to a Scottish Parliament, a Welsh Assembly and a (city regional) directly elected Mayor and Assembly for London may prove to be the most significant feature of the Government's overall approach.

But the public service improvement agenda is also important. However, when the Government came to the issue of public service improvement, it plainly considered that change would be most effectively delivered by strengthening accountability to the centre through plans and targets. The assumption was that these would alter the attention of institutional leaders (local politicians or agency chief executives) and deliver substantive change in the short term.

This approach became more complex when the 'silo' approach to service organisation and delivery came under attack. The shift towards 'joining up' at the same time as extolling the virtue of national plans, priorities and targets certainly demands smarter strategists (to produce the plans and ensure their coherence with other plans with which they need to interrelate). And as the following quote, from a recent Performance & Innovation Unit Report shows, this lesson is still being learnt:

> There are too many Government initiatives, causing confusion; not enough co-ordination; and too much time spent negotiating the system rather than delivering ... area-based initiatives, conceived and managed separately by individual central Government Departments, have created a very substantial bureaucratic burden for those on the ground.
>
> (Cabinet Office, 2000b)

It is axiomatic that small client groups who require complex packages of services (often involving multiple assessment from differing 'expert professionals' working in separate institutions) would greatly benefit through more joined-up service delivery. And a key lesson of the Cabinet Office's Social Exclusion Unit is that focused attention on small but intensely needy client groups requires combined and not simply coordinated action. For many people with severe needs seem to occupy the gaps or the overlaps between service providers and, in consequence, get poor service. But joining up is not a panacea for dealing with poor performance. Join a mediocre service with an average one and the service will worsen. Similarly, a poorly thought-through service strategy allied to an ineffective one will amplify the waste of people's time and talents. The call for more holistic solutions was correct. But the efforts of connecting every service activity with other activities can, too, often result in strategic constipation and can blunt the drive to action.

But the Government has not only been concerned with effecting change in sub-national institutions in the UK. It has also placed considerable emphasis on modernising the 'Whitehall machine' itself. A number of changes are notable in the shape of the Whitehall machine. For local government, the most notable feature was the early creation of the large Department of the Environment, Transport and the Regions (DETR) alongside a gradual development of functions in Government Regional Offices (most recently with the insertion of Home Office staff working to Regional Crime Directors). Other notable changes include the development of the No. 10 Policy Unit, and the bolstering of the Cabinet Office (although falling short of the much expected Prime Minister's Department) with the Social Exclusion Unit, the Performance & Innovation Unit and the Office of the E-Envoy.

These developments have provided a rich seam for academic mining, with over 20 major research projects being completed on the changing landscape and dynamics of Whitehall. The key findings of the Economic and Social Research Council (ESRC) Whitehall Programme point to a new twist in the development of the 'New Public Management' paradigm. Four points are notable here in terms of their relevance to local government. First, a clear shift from government to governance: from strengthening accountability vertically within institutions, to widening accountability horizontally across public sector institutions. Second, a context where politicians struggle to exercise 'more control over less'. Third, the continuation of the process whereby the state at national level is 'hollowed out' of both informal authority and formal functions (arising from the twin pressures of increasing globalisation and increasing public demands for governmental devolution). And, finally, the researchers point to the limitations of policy networks to deliver accountable public services.

Policy networks are proposed by some as the best solution to the problem of fragmentation in service delivery as well as the best basis for joining up services at the local level. Policy networks have grown with the recognition that simple solutions for complex problems are wrong and that messy or fuzzy approaches have a greater chance of success. No one institution is 'in charge' of solving these complex problems on their own and so they search for a way to collaborate to solve the problems together.

At some levels and for some functions (particularly at the regional level in respect of, say, transport planning and economic development), policy networks solve some of the practical problems of achieving a shift away from government to governance. But they, nonetheless, possess several important deficiencies when it comes to resolving problems at, say, the local level. For example, networks can be closed to outsiders, unrepresentative and unaccountable. They often serve private (or sectional) interests, they can be very difficult to steer and, finally, they can be inefficient in that enforced collaboration between agencies in networks causes delay. But networks also have real advantages. In particular, they work in circumstances where markets and hierarchies fail. Thus, we may need to recognise that new governance networks will have their own limits – if not in respect of their effectiveness in coordinating services in complex settings, then in their capacity to ensure public accountability of these services.

However, the reality of operating in a world where power is shared between agencies and where no one institution is singly responsible for solving specific social problems (such as crime, poor health, unemployment or environmental decay) requires the development of broad leadership skills. This is another of the arguments underlying the elected mayor debate, for, if mayors wish to be successful, they will need to be seen as leading a locality and not just the institution of the Council.

5 DELIVERING GREATER PRODUCTIVITY AND IMPROVING PERFORMANCE

The present watchwords of the political debate are 'delivery', 'productivity' and 'performance': delivery needs to be responsive, timely, efficient, modern and seamless; productivity needs to be heightened; while performance needs to be consistent, reliable and assured. But things that are simple to exhort sometimes seem impossible to effect. And, while all political parties use these words (with their own differing emphases) and wish the change, it is the Government of the day that has the responsibility for leading the change.

And there can be little doubt that, after four years, the present Government has substantially recast the terrain for public services. Their focus on modernised frontline service delivery (using web-enabled technologies and the like) and targeted initiatives to combat persistent social problems (like the rough sleepers initiative, the national drug and cancer 'tsars' and so on) is beginning to be effective in specific areas. Their central problem is how to achieve systemic change in the wider public sector.

A key concern has, understandably, been how best to improve public sector productivity. To investigate this issue, the Treasury established a cross-sectoral panel and published its interim findings in September 2000 (Productivity Services Panel, 2000). The report starts with a stark statistical truth: that a 3 per cent rise in productivity by the public sector could free up over

£6 billion per annum which could then be reinvested in services making a significant contribution to Britain's economic performance. However, this 3 per cent rise will not come about by accident; it requires a step change in the management of productivity in public services, for it assumes substantial 'X-inefficiency' in the public sector.

Theoretically, X-inefficiency occurs where an organisation fails to get the maximum possible output from the inputs it uses or to produce its output from the minimum use of inputs. X-inefficiency implies that there is 'slack' in the organisation. And, thus, for politicians and managers to achieve higher levels of productivity, they need to operate within an assumption that the public institution they are responsible for has moderately high levels of X-inefficiency. If they really believe there is no slack in their organisation, they will lack the confidence and credibility to build productive change.

Too often in the public sector, productivity gains are assumed as dormant, ready to be realised through purposive management action. And, in this regard, clarity in concepts is as important as clarity in objectives. In organisational theory, there is an important distinction between appraising internal efficiency and external efficiency. Conventionally, 'productivity' is the measure (inputs to outputs) of the internal efficiency of an organisation. However, the benefit of organisational performance to others is a measure of its external efficiency (or its effectiveness). And it is this wider benefit that is now usually encompassed within a broader understanding of the term 'productivity'.

However, the political and policy arguments contain a great deal of confusion; for productivity can be said to increase when costs remain stable, while output (or service coverage and/or quality) increases. And productivity can also be said to increase when costs decline but output (or service coverage and/or quality) at least stays stable. In local government, both are often required (although seldom explicitly stated) and this is encapsulated in the phrase, 'more for less'. Importantly, increases in service productivity can be achieved without any increase in service quality.

A key measure in choosing between options for productivity enhancements is the proportionality in the change of inputs to outputs: a term referred to by economists as 'returns to scale'. This describes the relation between a proportional change in inputs to a productive process and the resulting proportional change in outputs. If output rises by a smaller percentage than inputs, there are said to be 'decreasing returns to scale'; if it's larger, it is 'increasing returns to scale'; if the same, it is 'constant returns to scale'. This is an important concept when considering investing marginal resources for change in an organisation. Will a 5 per cent increase in labour resources in a service result in a 5 per cent increase in productivity? Hardly ever. Indeed, in many services, it is often new activities rather than more of the same activities that produce added value to service users.

In their consideration of productivity across the public sector, the Treasury's Productivity Panel discussed the need for:

- strengthened leadership to ensure clarity and focus on service improvement
- better techniques and strategies for tackling variations in performance
- measuring what matters, by prioritising and rationalising public sector targets
- a sharper focus on customers, who rightly expect better public services
- improved rewards and reinforcements for public servants.

Within these five areas, they then recommended a number of more specific actions, including the need to do the following:

- Build much greater organisational capacity for performance management, to help leaders develop effective systems and achieve the necessary supporting cultural change.

- Ensure all targets and measures in public services flow from Public Service Agreements and Service Delivery Agreements (PSAs and SDAs). The Panel did recognise, however, that the range of performance measures and targets in the public sector can contradict each other and confuse both staff and customers.

- Ensure stretching targets are set for raising the productivity of all public services and, where possible, differentiating targets to ensure performance is raised towards the standards of the best.

- Implement incentive schemes, which include financial rewards for exceeding PSA/SDA targets. And, finally, the Panel argued that the Government should provide the financial freedoms necessary for such incentives to work effectively.

This form of performance framework is not new. But the clarity of its presentation is welcome and the Treasury's attempt to promote productivity and performance improvement across the public sector rather than simply through Whitehall is also welcome. The Treasury's focus is usually on the plans, targets and agreements but it is notable that the Panel's recommendations start with building organisational capacity. This is a very positive development in Government thinking.

The essence of continuous quality improvement can be found in the process control approach advocated by Deming. He argued that four processes needed to be controlled: improved product design, elimination of product defect, elimination of waste and improvements in overall processes. He stressed the need for hard metrics (now called smart targets). But Deming realised that quality improvement processes involved more than process control: he argued that they also needed better people management, knowledge sharing and inspired leadership.

This is only now becoming acceptable wisdom in Government, following hard upon an overly quantitative planning and targeting approach. Plans are necessary but sufficient. The tradition of requiring public institutions to produce plans is a conventional route to promoting change across the public sector. But plans (however complex in their constitutive elements) are simply descriptions of intended actions. From the perspective of an institution's leadership, they show third parties that operational activity is purposeful and directive, and that available assets and resources are aligned to achieve stated objectives. They may also be helpful in mobilising people within the institution to act purposefully (people tend to follow those who can demonstrate some authoritative appreciation of the general direction in which the organisation is headed).

The limits to planning

One of the main purposes of a plan is to convince others that you know what you are doing and to show that the public resources at the institution's disposal are going to be used responsibly and with social purpose. But, as Kierkergaard said, the irony of life is that it is lived forward and yet best understood backwards. Less philosophically, we can see from Figure 2 that, when 'realised plans' are examined, they are as much a consequence of

Figure 2 The strategic planning process

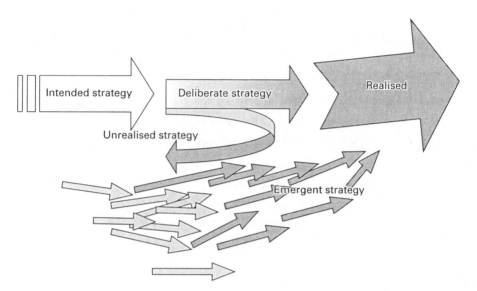

emergent properties (opportunities, innovations, unplanned incidents) as the result of intentional or deliberate plans of senior management. By corollary, much of what is intended is unrealised.

Strong strategic planning is a weakness in an organisation if it is too rigid in application. If this point is thought overly theoretical or fanciful, consider for just a moment the issue referred to in the opening paragraphs of the introduction to this paper: the fuel distribution crisis. In late 1999, local government was knee-deep in contingency planning to ensure its preparedness for the Y2K problem. This was contingency planning at its most advanced. It involved inter-organisational scenario planning and simulation exercises across the length and breadth of the country. Auditors checked the plans and the Government's Regional Offices had senior 'readiness teams' assessing each locality's plans. And yet, when a real crisis emerged, only nine months later the trusty Y2K contingency plans were shown to assume that everyone could get fuel!

This example shows, however, the essence of planning. For the overall benefit of planning (whether of a strategic or more operational variety) is that it demands of those doing the planning explicitly to calculate in advance anticipated risks under different courses of action. Moreover, it requires an explicit calculation, again in advance, of the likely consequences of the decisions made. For, in the public sector, no decisions are 'consequence-free' and the risks (to the public as well as to the Treasury) require detailed calculation. Therefore, a key issue to be addressed when determining the prevailing calculations for any given service plan is the central trade-offs between financial (cost-benefit or savings-harm analysis) and service objectives.

Another problem with plan-based approaches is that so much of the Government's agenda is experimental. We simply don't know what type and manner of intervention will best prevent criminal activity among young men or improve their exam results at school. That is why the Cabinet Office's Centre for Management and Policy Studies is promoting an 'evidence-based' approach to policy development. But a central difficulty for Government is that it is expected to operate in the now, to have all the answers to all describable problems and to be ahead of the news and media rhythm. The Government is thus caught in the dilemma of desperately wanting to promote evidence-based policies but not having the space and time to wait for the evidence to appear. For example, Health Action Zones seem to be integrating into mainstream health service activity long before any systemic lessons could have been learnt from their intended experimentation. Action is needed today; evidence comes tomorrow!

These are not arguments to abandon planning nor evidence-based approaches. Planning is not futile, it is essential. And policy development is always incremental; once new evidence shows that certain activities have little or no effect they should be ceased and resources deployed on other activities that offer greater promise. But the key point is that basing one's action on plans and empirical evidence may be necessary, but it does not guarantee success.

The rise of performance funding

It is perhaps not surprising that the plan-based approach to effecting change is seen as, at best, only a partial solution. For conventional wisdom dictates that it is when money talks that people act. This leads all governments to consider how best to 'incentivise' public institutions. The theory is that the prospect of more money tends to make people alert and draws their attention. Even those who favour an 'institutionalist' approach to understanding the public sector would encourage governments to effect change through funding. For, in this approach, the 'principal' (or in other words the Government as funder) will be able to stimulate the 'agent', or the service provider, to change course to one favoured by the principal.

So, why not use the promise of more money to get the public sector to change? This strategy has an honorable pedigree: he who pays the piper calls the tune. And, from time to time, it works well. Leaders of institutions want their organisations to prosper and grow, and the prospect of additional money to do new things may make them realign their resources and do things differently. From the perspective of Government, this approach makes a lot of sense; hence, the development of competitive bid based processes (most developed in urban regeneration but increasingly used in other service programme areas).

As indicated earlier, the Treasury's review of productivity has led it to adopt a performance contract model for relations within

29

Government: using the PSA or SDA framework. These began as resource and performance contracts between the Treasury and government departments to ensure that, once the first round of spending reviews was complete, departments got 'money in exchange for modernisation'. They are now being piloted in 20 local Councils. The idea is simple. Councils will 'negotiate' a dozen or so performance targets with the DETR (who now have the responsibility for implementing the scheme). These targets will be a blend of key national service targets with a few local service targets. In return for achieving performance above a set standard, the Councils will benefit from operating in a slightly more permissive environment (in the context of agreed 'freedoms and flexibilities') and with a financial bonus of up to 2.5 per cent of revenue support grant, payable after a three-year period.

This new approach is an undoubted incentive to Councils to find local solutions to national problems and to attract resources into their areas. However, the task of achieving these performance improvements is not simple. By shining a light on a particular subject, management attention becomes more focused and operational activity ought to become more sharply delivered, thereby increasing productivity and performance. However, there are at least two confounding issues.

First, it is seldom clear which operational activities will optimise outputs or performance outcomes (hence the trend to find 'evidence-based' approaches to implementation). And, on close inspection, prospective performance 'targets' are little more than operational indicators accumulated over the past few years. Second, there is the differential 'returns to scale' problem referred to above. It would be an imprudent authority that focused its actions on areas that produced only decreasing or even constant returns to scale (i.e. where output rises by the same percentage or indeed a smaller percentage than the increase in inputs or resources involved). That noted, the local PSA approach currently offers both national and local government the best chance for focusing resources and management attention on problems that require concerted action.

The local PSA approach could become a form of output-oriented 'balanced scorecard' for local government. A balanced set of 12 performance targets could be selected to reflect the totality of purposes of local government (the present format produces a more selective and partial list). The scorecard idea was developed in the mid-1990s to assist companies to break free from the classic fiscal measures of productivity and performance (return on capital employed, return on investment, return on total assets and so on). But, while it has potential for wide use in the public sector, to date its use has been very limited (principally in Sweden). The novelty in the local PSA approach is that marginal future funding is to be related to performance across a dozen indicators.

An important discussion paper produced jointly by the Institute of Public Policy Research (IPPR) and the New Local Government Network (NLGN) proposes, in the context of a more vibrant 'new localism', a Partnership Contract approach for performance funding. The centre-piece of this idea is to blend PSA and beacon approaches with the new requirement for Councils to produce multi-sectoral community strategies. Building on the French *contract-de-ville* approach, the authors of *Towards a New Localism* (Filkin *et al.*, 2000) argue forcefully for dramatic performance-related funding (with performance rewards of some £8 million additional rate-support grant per annum rather than the £2 million per annum as with the present PSA pilots). The idea, if it can be connected with an element of needs-based funding, has considerable merit and, given the quantum of resources proposed, would certainly prompt more wide-scale change than that encouraged by the existing (and somewhat disparate) approaches. However, it may well be that the Partnership Contract model proposed by the authors contains several (but not all) of the deficiencies of the 'network solution' referred to above in terms of ambiguous accountabilities and the difficulties of co-opting special interests onto a general purpose partnerships.

Extrinsic incentives will always have a positive effect. But they will also have a decay rate. Those of us with money to spare can all 'incentivise' our teenage children to get good GCSE scores. But we also know that, for them to succeed in the long run, they will need their own intrinsic motivation. And that is the central topic of this paper. How do you encourage change from within? What are the best approaches that can be taken to ensure enduring progress in local government? External incentives are needed. But, to sustain progress, an intrinsic passion for community development and organisational improvement is required to alter the current state of local government.

The local state we're in

Perhaps the best appraisal of the state of local government (while awaiting the end of year reports from the Audit Commission's Best Value Inspectorate) stems from the Improvement & Development Agency's (IDEA's) peer review process. This not only has the merit of being recent, it is also credible to local government as the judgements passed were by peer review teams.

After completing 44 reviews, the IDEA has reported on the overall picture of change across local government. Albeit a small sample (about 10 per cent of UK local government), it is the product of reasonably in-depth peer appraisal and as such represents a significant and fairly reliable portrait of local government.

Each Council was assessed against an 'ideal type' benchmark. The benchmark involved three broad domains: leadership, democratic and community engagement, and performance management. Each domain was itself comprised of five constituent elements. And the task of the peer review team was to appraise their assigned Council against three normative levels that were set for each element. For example, the leadership domain is composed of five elements of which 'vision and strategy' is the first. The IDEA normative benchmark has three levels for this element (scoring 1, 3 or 5). Table 2 shows the scores across the full set of elements in the benchmark.

Table 2 The IDEA normative benchmark scores

	1st level (%)	3rd level (%)	5th level (%)
Leadership			
Vision and strategy	45	44	11
Change management	44	56	–
Motivation	30	63	7
Innovation and creativity	33	60	7
Alliance building	22	59	19
Democratic and community engagement			
Democratic representation	22	74	4
Scrutiny	74	26	–
Customer and citizen focus	26	74	–
Communication	22	74	4
Consultation and participation	19	62	19
Performance management			
Planning and review	52	48	–
People management	26	74	–
Project management	37	63	–
Systems and process management	55	41	4
Financial management	37	56	7

Source: Murphy (2000).

From their analysis, the IDEA identified six areas for improvement. Three of these related to supporting political change. Three others related more to organisational and managerial change. The actual areas identified for change were as follows:

- Political leadership needs to be exercised more through dialogue than through formal meetings.

- Decision-making processes require the same challenge as service provision.

- Councillors' roles need to be supported in new ways outside the Town Hall.

- Organisational development is needed in many Councils to change cultures.

- Project management needs to be integrated into mainstream management.

- The strategies and plans required of Councils need to be joined up.

The IDEA appears to have arrived at its conclusions cautiously. The low numbers of Councils attaining the highest level in those elements that are central to the purpose of local government (such as democratic representation) could be described as shocking. Admittedly, local government was assessed as performing broadly well on partnership building, as the highest scores were attained in those elements of consultation and alliance building. These are elements central to partnership development. But the scale of what has to be achieved in improving overall leadership and delivering focused performance management is evident from these results. The IDEA rightly points to some excellent practice and the overall reasonable standards achieved. But their results also highlight the peaks that have to be climbed to achieve the dramatic changes that are needed in local government.

Following on from this diagnosis, it can be said that progressive change is needed on three dimensions in local government.

- First, progressive change in service design and delivery.

- Second, progressive change in local politics and governance.

- Third, and in support of the first two changes, it is vital that there is concomitant progressive change in management and organisation.

This paper will address the issues involved in the first two of these and then examine in a little more depth the issues involved in achieving progressive management change.

6 PROGRESSIVE CHANGE IN SERVICE DELIVERY

There is insufficient space here to cover the entire range of service change required in local government, as all local authority services require modernising to one extent or another. There are three essential and complementary routes to quality and effective service delivery: improved service design, improved process management (financial, project management, quality assurance, etc.) and better people management.

But, in local government, 'best value' is the dominant process whereby Councils are rethinking and reshaping their services. Best value is not a regime of specified and enforced service tendering, more an imposed ethic of continuous improvement. Authorities are required to undertake fundamental reviews of all functions and services within a five-year period ending in 2005 and with consecutive five-year cycles thereafter. The objective of these reviews is to make a real and positive difference to services on the ground. In addition to achieving the objective of making a positive difference, authorities will need to demonstrate they have complied with requirements around the 4 'C's of Challenge, Consult, Compare and Compete.

Each fundamental review must produce an action plan with details of how its aims are to be turned into practice. This will include clear performance targets and indicators with processes for monitoring and reporting progress. Outcomes and action plans from each review must be included in the following performance plan.

The Best Value Inspectorate will make its assessment of whether an authority is providing a best value service based on two judgements. First, it will assess performance in relation to the best practice as well as a practical 'reality check' on the state of current operational service delivery. The judgement will then be conveyed through the form of a star rating whereby three stars indicate a service in the top/best quartile and no stars in lowest/worst quartile. Second, it will form a judgement, as a result of the review, as to whether the service will improve. This will. range from 'Yes', 'Probably', 'Unlikely' to 'No' (see Figure 3). In extreme cases of failing services assessed as poor with no prospect of improvement, the Audit Commission will refer Councils to the Secretary of State who then, subject to proper process, has powers of intervention.

This approach is elegantly simple and will undoubtedly be beneficial to a wider public understanding of the relative quality

Figure 3 The Best Value Inspectorate's approach to assessment

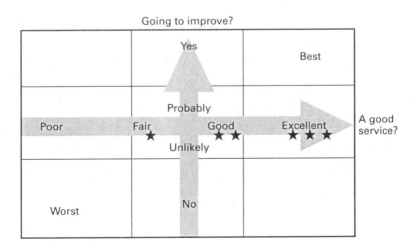

of local government services. But, perhaps unsurprisingly, Councils have already found that the approach has become a little swamped in process. This is partly local government's own fault for reviewing their services in too small chunks and enveloping themselves in disproportionately costly reviews. But it is also because the best value regime has incorporated too little from earlier total quality management, continuous improvement and business process redesign approaches.

Those Councils with a non-ideological approach to securing service provision and with systemic approaches to quality management, investment and training in people learn least (if anything) from the best value regime. Project managing the inspectors, for too many, takes precedence over process control managing the services. Given the requirement to meet the disciplines of the Audit Commission's inspection regime, it is to be expected that many Councils approach best value in this defensive way at this stage.

The best value approach should deliver significant service change in the short term, although other factors (such as e-business solutions) may well prove to have a more dramatic impact on services over the medium and longer term. Managerially, perhaps the most important aspect of best value is the requirement for fundamental challenge of service purpose and provision (what elsewhere in the public sector is often referred to as a 'prior options' review). Indeed, the change of language from providing services to 'securing' services has itself resulted in a changed mindset with Councils about purpose and role.

Beyond these reviews it is vital that management focuses attention on how to improve the productivity of all Council services, for, with 20 per cent of services (by volume) being subject to in-depth reviews each year, it is a truism that 60 per cent of services will not be subject to in-depth reviews for at least two years. And two years is too long to wait to improve the productivity of 60 per cent of Council services.

Managers need to develop robust and rigorous approaches to performance assessment. The best value performance indicators are a starting point; they do not describe the totality. A comprehensive approach to performance assessment involves a triangulated approach where hard metrics on costs, value and service performance are measured on three dimensions:

- *comparative*: where performance is measured against the performance of a relevant sample of other service providers

- *normative*: where performance is measured against a norm, standard or target

- *ipsative*: where performance is measured against previous personal best performance.

In practical terms, achieving purposive increases in productivity requires a detailed understanding of the mix of labour, capital and technology for each service activity (such as social work, refuse collection or environmental health) and assessing the merits of alternative innovative approaches to changing this mix. Redesigning a service to lower its cost base and/or enhance its value added is central to service planning in local government. And the best value regime encourages both a fundamental reassessment of service purpose and provision, and a culture of continuous improvement.

However, the current conventions imply that all that is needed is a target and a system for reviewing performance. The 'black box' in the analysis is what managers and staff in local government actually do to increase the volume or sharpen the focus of activity to achieve the desired output and hence the intended outcomes. The planned target and the review process are simply the stage on which service performance is enacted. Of themselves, they do nothing (beyond casting spotlights) to increase productivity. They may focus management attention on what is important. But that is all.

Real productivity change stems from any number of managerial strategies: from tighter cost controls; from better alignment of resources; from enhanced motivation amongst staff; from innovation and entrepreneurship; from different mixes of labour, capital and technology; and from redefining the boundary between service provider and service user. And, while innovation in the private sector can be said to stem from market pressures and the prospect of imminent failure, the public sector has a more contentious embrace with innovation. It is pivotal to increasing productivity but it is not systemically developed. A recent appraisal of innovation in government departments by the National Audit Office (2000) showed the importance of improved risk management. Their report identified four types of risks: financial risk; project risk; compliance risk; and the risk of missing opportunities. Innovation and explicit risk management are as central in delivering productivity changes in local government.

But the scale of service change required in local government is greater than that which derives from improved productivity or the continuous improvement ethic of best value. Social care services need reshaping to be relevant to new and emerging needs and to mesh more effectively with health care and other related services. Education services need to be smart and effective in delivering change in schools and in supporting schools proportionate to risk and performance. And environmental services need to embrace new approaches to ecological management and urban design.

The style of local government services needs to change as much as the scope and scale of them. For services need to be attuned to diversity within the citizen and customer base, and their design and delivery need to be assured against both institutional racism and disability discrimination. And, in local government, where service is expected to be tailored to local circumstance, it is important to ensure that the style and substance of service are relevant and appropriate to the needs of people of differing ethnic origins.

Perhaps the best prospect for progressive service change occurs when service users are drawn to the centre of the design and delivery of services. It is only when the changing needs of all service users are intimately factored into service redesign that services have a chance to retain their relevance.

The e-agenda

Moreover, all services need to adapt to the new electronic channels for delivery. Service users now have their own 'four Cs': they can:

- Come in
- Correspond
- Call, or
- Click.

And increasingly they will opt for the latter. For, despite the persistence of a digital divide (forecast to flatten out over the coming decade), the growth in Internet ownership at home is considerable. Citizens demand service information and many service transactions on a 24-hour, seven-day-a-week basis. The increasing use of e-service channels to deliver service will not only increase choice to consumers but also enable local government dramatically to lower its cost base. However, as with all service change, new channels cost money and costs will only be lowered overall if traditional service channels are, at least partly, decommissioned. In other words, Councils cannot maintain all of their existing corporate estate, administrative buildings and service facilities while building new electronic channels of service delivery, for overall costs could mushroom rather than shrink.

Councils need urgently to adopt sensible e-business strategies that take full account of the range of services for which they are responsible. These e-business strategies need to show not only how services can be reconfigured on a lower cost base and how they are accessible across a broader range and time zone (24/7), but also how, where practicable, they are personally tailored and promote customer autonomy and independence. In inner urban areas, ownership at home of Internet-accessible devices grew to four in ten of all households by the end of 2000. On the back of this growth in demand, the impact of web-enabled technologies on public service delivery is likely to be dramatic over the longer term. Citizens will be enabled to gain information about any public service through personalised portals and to transact for services over the Internet. The current targets for placing local government services on-line (100 per cent by 2005) will, in time, no doubt be supplanted by even more rigorous targets for transactions and take-up.

The agenda of web-enabled government will not simply alter the cost base for public services but also move the public sector more towards an empowering and self-service approach. Importantly, web-enabled government offers citizens the prospect to cut through the apparent mess of policies and institutions to access public services directly. The boundaries within and between public institutions melt away in cyber-space and citizens can access services at their convenience. If services and information can be web-enabled, the potential for self-service is real and the political opportunities for redefining the relationship between citizen and state are considerable. At present, the adoption of the e-agenda in government lags some way behind the private sector. And this trend may well continue. But this agenda offers unique advantages for a fresh approach to public service.

But it is not just services that need progressive change; so, too, do politics and governance at the local level.

7 PROGRESSIVE CHANGE IN LOCAL POLITICS AND GOVERNANCE

The nature of change in modern society requires the reinvention of politics itself. In many ways, it can be said that the traditional politics of the local and the national (usually around contesting power over democratic institutions through election) is melting and a new politics of locally active but globally conscious is emerging.

At the local level, elected representatives continue to be questioned about their legitimacy to take some public interest decisions and their effectiveness when they do. This arises through a more informed citizenry whose experience of democratic institutions on the whole is one of disappointment. This is not a failing in elected representatives; it is the challenge of the current age.

The Government has two responses to this for local government. First, they wish to promote the direct 'at large' elections of mayors to raise the visibility, and hence the potential for accountability, between the elected and the electors. Second, they are examining the merits of alternative mechanisms of voting (postal voting, electronic voting, etc.) to enable barriers or inhibitors to voting to be reduced or eliminated.

These are both helpful innovations but what is needed is a more dramatic improvement in the connection between electors and their representatives. Only by influencing the vitality of local political culture will citizens be more motivated to vote and (as importantly) to get involved with public interest questions in their localities. At present, few people vote in local elections and the first-past-the-post electoral system at the local level results in perverse consequences in local government.

It is regrettable that very few leading local politicians in the two major parties have argued for changes to the local electoral system. The disproportionate results of local elections are quite shocking (with many Councils having 'deviations from proportionality' near their theoretical maximum). To date, very few Councils have seriously examined the effectiveness and appropriateness of alternative electoral systems for their area. The arguments for and against proportional representation at the local level tend to carry too many echoes of debates at the national level, and, yet, the issues at stake are radically different. At the local level, it is crucial that these issues are discussed, particularly when Councils are considering the directly elected mayor option – where the supplementary vote (SV) system will be used for the mayoral election.

Citizen engagement and local political change

Government-sponsored democratic innovations are helpful in prompting change. But citizen disengagement and voter apathy need more radical stimuli than are likely to arise through implementing marginal changes in voting arrangements. Importantly, civicism is not marginal to the development of a locality; it is central.

A key point for this discussion is the nature of the link between civil freedoms and economic or community development. In a recent and inspiring economic analysis, Amyarta Sen (1999) argues that, while 'basic civil and political rights are instrumental in providing security and protection for minorities … the general enhancement of civil freedoms is central to the process of development itself. Thus it is important to distinguish between the instrumental role of democracy from its constitutive role. Development is about expanding substantive freedoms: enhancing individual freedoms and the social commitment to help to bring it about.'

Applying his argument to the local level would mean that expanding civil freedoms (and the social commitment that stems from these freedoms) is central to the successful development of localities. Thus, if local government is to enhance the development of an area, it can only do so if it first promotes civicism in its area. This means that developments in local democracy are crucial to the economic development of localities. You can't have the latter without the former. And the starting point for building an informed and critical citizenry is with citizenship education.

However, the most notable political current of the modern age, and particularly as experienced at the local level, is the apparent apoliticisation of social change. Robert Putnam (2000) has comprehensively examined these trends in his impressive book *Bowling Alone*. At its broadest, he has produced an account of civic disengagement in modern America.

Putnam claims to document the overall decline of social reciprocity in American life. He charts declining attendance at church and declining engagement at work, with civic associations and in informal social networks. He points to the erosion of civic virtue that accompanies this general decline in social reciprocity and correlates these trends with decreasing political participation and voter turnout in elections. Putnam assesses these trends thoroughly and concludes that there are a number of forces at work. Most importantly, he writes of the 'civic generation' born before the 1930s whose life experience reinforced a strong mutuality and sense of civic virtue and which he counterposes to the differing value base of subsequent generations. But this generational change, for Putnam, is not the whole story. The past 50 years have witnessed some massive social changes. Not least of these has been a phenomenal increase in television viewing (for information and entertainment); very substantial urban and suburban sprawl; and the pace and scale of competition in market economies further increasing the pressures upon people's time and money. Little wonder that people, increasingly, 'bowl alone'.

Intuitively it seems that Putnam's conclusions for American society resonate with British experience. It would be fascinating to test his thesis in the context of British social trends. In particular, the connections between local social capital, the trends in party alignment, political activism and civic engagement merit in-depth study in the British context.

However, it would be wrong simply to assume that there has been a straightforward tailing off of civic engagement in Britain. In every locality, there will be many hundreds of active citizens contributing to the life of their community. And, in many ways, there will be more people engaged as active citizens now than in the past. But this involvement is most likely to have the character of a particularised or specific interest (school governing bodies, park user groups, traffic calming lobby groups, etc.). And the challenge to those engaged with wider political action at the local level is to guide people from particularised involvement with local issues to a more generalised involvement in the civic affairs of their locality.

There are at least four types of progressive change required in local politics.

- First, better engagement between active citizens, civil society and political parties is needed at the local level.

- Second, a healthier competition for office and contest for leadership is needed locally (perhaps for far fewer positions).

- Third, improved decision making on public interest issues locally and more inclusive governance arrangements are required.

- Fourth, new styles of political leadership are needed to deal with the complex governance networks in localities and the developing requirements of overlapping partnership vehicles (for both regeneration and service delivery).

The first of these changes is crucial and needs to be addressed by the political parties. They need to attend to the culture of political engagement in localities. It is not an issue of organisation (ward-based political structures, supporting Parliamentary constituency structures, supporting district-wide structures and so on). It is about the political culture within localities. How open and engaging are political parties? How do they relate to particularised social movements in their area? And how do they go about articulating a future vision for their area (is it an internal discussion within their party or is it more inclusively drawn)?

These questions are beyond the scope of this paper. But they need answering by all political parties. If local political action is to carry wide public support, leadership at the local level needs to be engaging not elite-focused. In particular, political parties need to be seen by the wider public to be focused less upon formal internal debates and more upon articulating local community needs.

Modernising local governance

Following the Local Government Act 2000, the enforced separation of a small political executive from a larger oversight and scrutiny group of councillors is precipitating formal change within Councils' governance arrangements. However, while the change seems considerable when viewed from the inside, from the outside it seems that change is more stylistic than substantive. The mass movement of Councils towards the cabinet and leader model at a very early stage is a worrying trend. Cabinets that are little more than the old Policy & Resources Committee, writ small, are likely to become cabinets made of veneer. Without some alteration to traditional party whipping in local government (and particularly in Councils where single party executives are in force), they may be little more than decorative changes to the nature of existing decision making. And Councils need to ensure that they are not merely pouring old wine into new bottles.

One of the central themes of this paper is the importance when jumpstarting any change of widespread dissatisfaction with current arrangements. Any political change must therefore begin with dissatisfaction amongst the participants (elected councillors and potential councillors) with current arrangements. A smug or complacent attitude will be the undoing of local government, or will, at the least, lead to even further erosion in its legitimacy.

So what are the current arrangements, and are they satisfactory? Well, once every four years (more often in some places), just three in ten people turn out to vote in elections. In the main, they have a choice between three or four people who have been selected to stand in small party meetings of ten or so people. A party whose candidates win one-half of the votes cast can find that they win nearly all the seats and those elected then decide among themselves who leads on what. Don't misunderstand the point; local democracy is by far the best way for public interest issues to be decided. The issue is how to improve the democratic bases and electoral processes of the present system.

At the local level, it would be difficult to argue that throughout the country political parties are healthy and that the contest for office is real and full-blooded. This is not to deny the immense contribution made by many thousands of people in their local communities. Nor is it a denial of the very real contest for community leadership in some localities. The efforts of councillors and active citizens (and the personal sacrifice of those concerned) are astonishing given the character of the rewards they face. And a considerable number of councillors have genuine and authentic roots in, and connections with, the communities they represent. But nonetheless, and seen as a whole, the 'selectorate' which chooses people to stand for elected office is relatively small in number; and the contest for office is neither universally full scale nor fierce.

One key change that is required must involve reducing the numbers of councillors on Councils. The *Guardian's* local government correspondent, Peter Hetherington, recently argued, in a paper published by the Local Government Association, for a reduction in the numbers of councillors by two-thirds. This is a serious proposal that requires wide attention. Reductions in councillor numbers need to be seriously considered.

At a stroke, this will increase competition for office and strengthen the health of political activity at the local level. There is little point in shoring up local government if the political parties that contest office have neither the numbers nor the energy to mount local campaigns. The drive for directly elected mayors (or others elected 'at large') will undoubtedly raise the visibility of politicians as well as increase the contest for office. And, while visibility is not a synonym of accountability, it is a prerequisite.

However, this change is not of itself enough. The 'separation of powers' achieved through the Government's new proposals will require substantive changes in political practice to work.

First, there is arguably too much party discipline involved in local government. Political parties are crucial to bringing order to the competition for ideas and values in wider society. But, given the sorts of decisions made at the local level, is strict party discipline really necessary across the full range of Council activities? As an example, it can be argued that the prevailing tendency for Councils to opt for 'single party' executives works against transparent conduct of public life at local level. It is striking that Councils are obliged to consult with their communities in great depth about the options for governance change but (with some notable exceptions) very few are consulting their public on this aspect of their proposed governance changes. These issues present very real challenges to political parties at the local level.

But, as with national politics, local councillors struggle to exercise greater control over fewer functions. In some respects, local elections enable a contest for office without power while powers are exercised elsewhere in the public realm. Consider the smaller District Councils in England. If they have transferred their housing stock to a registered social landlord, it is likely that they will have a staff of some 250, an annual revenue budget of about £12 million and yet about 50 councillors! Why? Secondary schools in the same area will employ more staff, have bigger budgets, be involved in deciding matters more socially and politically significant (than, say, local environmental maintenance) and yet be governed by lay people in their own time and at their own expense. With a politician to officer ratio of 1:5 in these Councils there is ample scope for micro-management by local politicians and for role confusion between managers and politicians. But this issue is not confined to District Councils. There are many examples of large unitary Councils being ineffective because the relationship between politicians and managers is unclear or unhealthy.

In short, the Government's new legislation precipitates change. But changes that will meet the basic requirements of the law are unlikely to meet the changing requirements of governance and civil society locally. These require much more substantive changes in the practice of political leadership in localities.

In many ways, far too much attention is being paid to the internal machinery of party politics on Councils (deciding who is in the executive, who sits on the scrutiny committees and codifying practice between the two). And, as a corollary, far too little attention is being paid to the wider needs of civil society.

Improving governance through making better decisions

One key aspect of improved governance is making better decisions. Decisions can be 'better' if they are made more swiftly, in a more informed manner and/or in a fashion that makes them more acceptable to the public. The principal source of policy advice to councillors is their professional advisers – their Council's senior managers. Officers need to ensure that councillors have the broadest base of policy advice, including views from service users, their advocates and citizens generally.

Unlike in central government, where policy advice is usually separated from operational management, Council officers are both service managers and policy advisers. This presents its own problems and managers need to be mindful of the intrinsic bias towards provider interests (in that they manage the services about which they advise councillors). The most senior Council officers need to move beyond the role of a service or professional advocate but they also need to eschew the disinterested and detached stance of the analyst. They need to be engaged with the issues while remaining unbiased and impartial. Professional report writing in local government can be caricatured as being composed of three styles:

- The 'light the blue touch paper and retire' report – this is where only one, professionally rational, option is advanced by officers who present it to politicians regardless of its acceptability and appropriateness.

- The 'on the one hand and on the other hand' style – this is where the one preferred option is presented but has equally balanced advantages and disadvantages (merits and demerits, costs and benefits) of sufficient detail so as to afford a political choice within the bounds of professional rationality.

- The 'Goldilocks' style – this is an altogether more manipulative approach where a 'too sweet' option is contrasted with a 'too sour' option and, in consequence, a third more acceptable option emerges through a process of rational compromise.

The nature of the arguments that are presented formally in reports has an obvious bearing on the quality of decisions made. But other less obvious factors also play their part. Viewed from the perspective of the participants to a meeting, the decisions of a meeting are public goods. The contribution that each participant can make towards achieving or improving these public goods will become smaller as the meeting becomes larger. Moreover, arithmetic underscores the problems in large numbers of people making decisions. Consider this. Two people have one relationship. Six people (the size of most management groups) have 15 relationships. A cabinet of ten has 46 relationships and a political group of 35 people has 598 relationships. It is hardly surprising, therefore, that relationships get frayed and problematic, and people feel left out.

This point supports the drive to smaller committees for conventional political decision making, although it is now also the case that new decision-conferencing software tools can support large groups of people to discuss and deliberate topical issues.

Moreover, while the machinery of Councils is changing, it is vital that the quality of public decision making and the quality of scrutiny improve the overall public accountability of local government. Legally, the Wednesbury principles govern the basis for local authority decision making. These refer to the importance of considering relevant factors while rejecting irrelevant ones. The creation of cabinet committees raises new issues for decision making. These cabinets should aim at improving the quality of their decisions, not simply the speed of their decision making.

Dialogue and deliberation are essential starting points for decisions and not stumbling blocks. Quality decisions in local government cabinets would benefit from a systematic approach that meets the following eight criteria:

1 Ensure that the right decision problem is being worked on.

2 Specify objectives.

3 Create imaginative options for solving the problem to hand.

4 Understand the consequences of each option.

5 Grapple with the inevitable trade-offs involved in each option.

6 Clarify the uncertainties.

7 Ensure the calculation of risk tolerance in the decisions being addressed.

8 Consider the linked nature of decisions.

This eight-step plan for better decisions is useful in any setting. Cabinets will need to begin to systematise their approach to decision making, to ensure thorough deliberation as well as to guarantee more streamlined decision processes. There is anecdotal evidence that cabinet committees are already leading to improved decision making in terms of issues being considered more corporately in authorities. The important issue arising now is to ensure that the more deliberative scrutiny aspects of the new governance structures add at least equal value to the public accountability of local Councils. The scrutiny aspect of governance needs to focus not only on its questioning role but also on its policy development function.

Purposeful community leadership

Decision making is not the sole purpose of political action at local level. Indeed, it could be argued that the decision needs of local government divert many active citizens away from more essential community action locally. However, it is the case that the possession of significant service functions (not the same as service provision) creates the capacity in local government to develop effective community leadership.

There is a growing need for councillors to deepen their community leadership skills. As a first step, it would be useful for Councils to focus on how best to develop the advocacy and representational skills of those councillors not in the executive.

Many are natural advocates for their locality. But very many also need help, assistance and development in this role.

Following this point, it becomes important to consider the issue of community leadership: how effective are councillors in promoting the civic good in their locality? As an illustration of what direction councillors could be leading their communities, let us consider the potential contribution they could make by using the social capital in their localities to rebuild civic engagement.

First, it is important to recognise the demands of modern life on local community. Community is not another name for paradise lost. The increasing pace of life and, crucially, its insecurities are creating a renewed call for community bonds to re-establish ties and attachments. But the protective security of community ought not to strangle the force of freedom, of autonomy of self-assertion or, in the modern phrase, 'the right to be yourself'. Group solidarity or social cohesion promotes a sense of security but, as one commentator argues, 'security without freedom equals slavery … while freedom without security equals abandonment' (Bauman, 2001).

This tension exists in any community – a tension between group solidarity and tolerance towards individuals and minorities. Communities with high social capital may display strong 'in-group' loyalties while being intolerant of 'outsiders' or simply people who have some difference from the majority in the community. Figure 4 attempts to codify community typologies along the two axes of solidarity (or fraternity) and tolerance (or liberty).

This typology could lead to the conclusion that a key role of local councillors is to promote behaviour and social conduct in the 'civic community' quadrant. This is where high social capital and high tolerance are promoted as the most ideal type for a community to follow. This analysis can help point to the central purpose of political leadership in localities, for councillors are not

Figure 4 Community typologies

	Low social capital	High social capital
High tolerance	Individualistic: you do your thing, I'll do mine	Civic community: all for one and one for all
Low tolerance	Anarchic: war of all against all	Sectarian community: Salem with 'witches'

there simply to decide between competing claims for public resources but also to provide leadership for the common or public good. This approach to promoting the civic community may be an ideal, but it is ideals that are the lynchpin of progressive change in local politics.

Political leaders need to reflect that, while communities that are supportive of their members can be said to be 'close', communities that are close can easily slip into being 'closed'. And that, in this globalising world, communities that succeed over the long haul will tend to be those that are open and that have as strong a desire to connect to the wider world as to establish connections within themselves.

A recent research exercise with large groups of citizens in three localities (Lewisham, Buckinghamshire and Hartlepool) examined the public view of the future of their communities (Rudat, 2000). This exercise, conducted by the New Local Government Network and the Office for Public Management, used visioning and deliberative techniques to elicit public attitudes towards local community and local government. The study concluded that the public are eager for new forms of citizen engagement and community activism to improve their localities, and they recognise that the governance of public issues in their area extends far beyond the boundaries of local government's functions and activities. The key conclusion of the research was that current processes of community engagement fail to tap the energies and ideas of people about how to improve their localities. The traditions of town hall meetings, councillor surgeries and community meetings are rapidly losing their relevance in the modern age.

These points help to illustrate aspects of community leadership that could be developed. There are many others that local politicians are developing and that the IDEA Leadership Academy is discussing with groups of councillors from across the country. The scope for these changes has been identified by a recent practitioner research study of 'active democracy' (Kirkham *et al.*, 2000), which concluded from research in 11 US cities that there was in the USA a stronger culture of citizen engagement than in the UK. This must become a central action point for local government.

Conventionally, civic education and enlightened understanding of the political process are things that arise from political competition and political parties supplying information to the wider electorate. But this is becoming more difficult for both citizens and political parties. Changes in the scale of government and the complexity of governance, and the explosion of the communication media present enormous challenges for citizens to become actively involved. It is therefore crucial that Councils have mechanisms and processes for informing, educating and engaging local citizens. A central question for political parties is how at the local level they can become a healthy vehicle for change.

A final point relevant here is the relationship between new forms of direct or deliberative democracy and conventional representative democracy. Too often, this is depicted as a trade-off. And too many elected representatives are overly anxious about the implications to their legitimacy of increased reliance on direct or deliberative democracy. For example, the increasing usage of citizens' juries and citizens' panels (and community referenda) should not be seen as a threat to the legitimacy of elected representatives. These new techniques need to be viewed as an important addition to democratic involvement rather than as a detraction from representative democracy.

Political change coupled with service change will create the conditions for wider change. But little will happen without change to the management or organisation of local government. And it is to this aspect that this paper now turns.

8 PROGRESSIVE CHANGE IN MANAGEMENT AND ORGANISATION

This chapter outlines wider trends in progressive managerial and organisational change in as far as these are relevant to local government. The specific need to reshape the relationship between management and politicians in local government is then considered and, finally, the paper sets out a four-stranded approach to implementing progressive change in management.

Outside of the claustrophobic character of discussion about local government management, the wider debate about organisations and their management is much more extensive and no less intense. Commentators and academics chart the changing trends in business practice and point to the substantial paradigmatic shifts in organisational theory. Each passing decade seems to be characterised by the adoption of a new suite of business processes, with knowledge management and creativity and innovation being the standard of the current times. A recent survey (by Bain & Co) that tracked the use of 20 business change strategies in over 470 companies clearly demonstrates this point (see Figure 5).

Figure 5 is not a map of passing fashions in organisational change but rather a reflection of the rise of the Internet and web-enabled technologies. The pervasive character of these technologies and the opportunities they offer to transform the cost base and supply chains of organisations is the dominant

Figure 5 Changes in the use of business change strategies

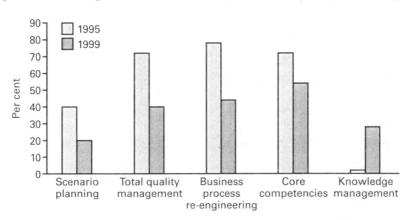

change process in business today. Hence, the rise of knowledge management approaches (for tapping the value within the organisation) and customer relations management approaches (for enhancing the interface with customers). And, as noted above, the rise of e-business solutions to traditional organisational questions of change is evident in local government as much as in the private sector.

But the fundamental tension between ensuring customer satisfaction with service quality while controlling (or containing) operational costs is not answered by e-business approaches. E-business approaches are essential at the current time as they offer the best prospect for transforming the cost, reach and personalisation of services. They provide new media and channels for service delivery. However, the fundamentals of quality management, business re-engineering and employee competencies remain as central organisational challenges to be tackled.

Successful managerial strategies for change are constituted in specific circumstances. And, in the private sector, it is the dynamic of changing business competitiveness that is the central factor driving change. Consider two examples in the private sector where the context for success or failure differs significantly. First, consider the strategies for small businesses in the high added value emerging information and knowledge markets (say, selling orchestration software for online music making). Second, consider the radically different strategy required for a large business seeking sustained competitive advantage for its products in a highly mature marketplace (say, selling toilet rolls). In these two examples, it can be seen that strategies for management action only make sense in the light of both a thorough appreciation of the potential of available resources and the opportunities in existing and prospective markets.

These examples show the diversity of the private sector. But a single Council contains just as much variety within itself: child-care nurseries, street cleaning, tax collection, housing maintenance and school improvement. Is it any wonder that prospective strategy formulation in local government is always vexed. On the one hand, there is the wisdom of Ashby's 'law of requisite variety'. This suggests that an organisation should contain sufficient variety within itself to meet the external environmental challenges it may face. This approach would result in organisations adopting complex and nuanced managerial strategies that balance activities carefully and that adopt complementary tactics to minimise risk. However, on the other hand are the equally plausible 'keep it simple' strategies. Complex approaches are understandable given the complexity of the world but they often go unimplemented. This complexity of approach is often characterised in both the private and the public sector by grand thinking but too little action. However, approaches that 'chunk' problems into manageable portions and attack them simply are much more likely to be implemented.

These tensions within strategy produce echoes in organisational design – with the classic dilemma of how best to balance the division of labour on single-purpose functions with the coordination and integration of these specialised functions.

These tensions of strategy and organisational design are highly pertinent in local government given the complexity of service demands and its traditions of specialised professional structures. And, in many ways, too much of local government retains the hallmarks of a guild professional organisation when the current demands it faces require more integrated and corporate approaches.

Trying to resolve these tensions has led to a wave of fashions in organising local government (and particularly the so-called 'top teams'). And, hopefully, it is only the most old-fashioned Councils that have retained the municipalist designations of yesteryear: Town Clerk, Borough Treasurer, or Borough Engineer. There was a passing fashion (which started in Brent and moved by way of Kirklees to Hackney and then Islington) with so-called portfolio or strategic Directors. This was a brave attempt to reshape the responsibilities of the Council's top team and to break up the old guild professionalism of the past. And, in different ways, it worked. But, where it failed, it was because the new system had not properly designed accountabilities within management. For, within Councils, it is crucial to design effective accountability for action and budgetary control between different managers. Organisations of several thousand people with blurred performance and budgetary accountability produce an awful lot of X-inefficiency! – fertile ground for lots of innovation and lots of unmanaged failure.

More recently, Councils have kept 'the baby' of corporate management while throwing out 'the bathwater' of over-rigid professionalism. Top management teams are beginning to be constructed around the executive service functions of the authority and not professional specialisms. But this is now being effected by the changes to political arrangements. The tradition of service departments, headed by a professional advocate accountable to a service committee, is being swept away. In its place, a corporate management board of more generic senior executives is now accountable both to a cabinet and to the wider Council. And, where the cabinet makes decisions collectively, this will work perfectly well. The real test, however, will be in those Councils where executive councillors will be making decisions as individuals.

This together with the external demands of a panoply of government sponsored Inspectorates is leading to a complete refocus for senior executives. Their role is vital for the overall leadership of the authority and, yet, the efforts of the Society of Local Authority Chief Executives (SOLACE) notwithstanding, their importance is overlooked in both legislation and the academic literature.

Moreover, with the reshaping of governance and the expectation that councillors will exercise executive authority individually, the precise role of senior managers in local government needs urgent attention. It will be exceedingly difficult to design corporate management responsibilities and align managerial executive responsibilities when political executives are composed of individual politicians who will be permitted in law to make decisions on their own account.

Thus, the nature of the relationship between managers and politicians needs urgent review given the pace of changes to governance structures subsequent to the Local Government Act 2000. The conventional relationship of adviser–decider or decider–implementer is insufficient for current purposes, let alone the changed environment. An American politician and public service academic (John Nalbandian of Kansas) has shown how politicians and managers operate within fundamentally different mindsets, using different models to interpret fairness and efficiency, and expressing their judgements in differing ways (see Table 3). Nalbandian argues that managers and politicians need to explain their differences more – not so as to diminish them but to avoid misinterpretation and mistrust.

His analysis is a very helpful starting point in building productive and healthy relations between managers and politicians. After all, theirs is the first order partnership for local government success. Anecdotal evidence appears to show that the most successful Councils have strong progressive politicians and strong progressive managers. In this regard it is worth quoting the recent paper, *Towards a New Localism*:

> These new systems of political leadership need to be seen as opportunities to increase political and managerial capacity rather than transferring it from one to another. Member–officer relationships must not be seen as a zero sum game.
>
> (Filkin *et al.*, 2000)

Table 3 Nalbandian's analysis of the relationship between politicians and managers

Characteristics	Politics	Management
Activity	Game	Problem solving
Players	Representatives	Experts
Conversation	'What do you hear?' stories	'What do you know?' reports
Pieces	Intangibles (symbols)	Tangibles (things)
Currency	Power	Knowledge
Dynamics	Conflict, compromise	Harmony, cooperation

Source: Nalbandian (1994).

The point of Nalbandian's analysis (he refers to the world of the politicians and the managers as being composed of two separate 'constellations of logic') is to encourage politicians and managers alike to appreciate each other's perspectives and realise that the public interest is advanced when both are effective. The partnership between senior managers and leading elected politicians needs to be honest and trust based if public services are going to develop in the public interest rather than in pursuit of sectional or vested interests.

In local government, the pivotal relationship between politicians and managers has been that between professional chief officers (usually service or client group advocates) and the chairs of service committees. The new model of political executive decision taking is serving to move Councils away from this bilateral approach towards a more corporate approach where a senior team of corporate managers relates (as a group) to a cabinet of politicians. However, the tendency to revert to old-style one-to-one relations between a 'lead member' and a 'lead professional' is strong. If the relations between politicians and managers revert to the bilateral approach, Councils will not leverage sufficient change in the relations between politicians and managers at this corporate level.

However the relations between politicians and managers develop, one thing is sure – develop they must. Politicians can bring energy, enthusiasm, a passion for the public interest and a genuine commitment to the public good. Managers can bring expertise and talent to achieving public purposes. If politicians relate to their managers and advisers in a captious manner, they will slow down progressive change in public services. And, if managers relate to politicians in an arrogant manner, they will not truly serve the public interest.

A productive relationship between managers and politicians is central to successful local government. But good relations do not of themselves lead to progressive change. Both sides need to be dissatisfied with the present if they want to deliver change.

From willing to delivering progressive change

"My mother always said to me that you have to put the past behind you before you can move on."

(Forest Gump)

In any setting, it's no good just willing change; it has to be delivered. To deliver change successfully requires those leading it to blend science with art. The science involves designing strategies, planning actions and marshalling resources, assets, money and people. This aspect of change is quantitative and disciplined. It requires those leading the change to be clear about their goals, to align and resource their plans of action, and to set out measures against which their 'success' can be judged. Among other things, this aspect of change emphasises the external context of incentives and penalties.

The artistic aspect of change is not amenable to quantification. Instead, it emphasises quality, purpose and balance. It uses emotion, symbols and personal example to inspire people to change direction. In short, it requires those leading the change to inspire and motivate others to achieve of their best. It assumes that 'when all is said and done people perform if they want to' and that the challenge is to tap the deeper yearnings of people to 'want to' so that higher performance is realised. Following this approach, effective institutional leaders help people to visualise a better future in ways that draw them inexorably towards it.

An organisation will only overcome its internal inertia when a critical mass of the people within it are themselves dissatisfied with things as they are, jointly agree on a long-term vision and have also agreed steps to getting there. Organisational inertia should never be underestimated. It is natural and human to want to resist change. In most cases, change is resisted passively. This point is crucial because too much attention is paid to those, usually small in number, who are actively resisting the changes proposed. It is the 'passive resisters' who need to be persuaded. And passive resistance can take many forms – from silent critics, cynics, 'naysayers' to low energy supporters.

The essential problem with these people is their sense of resignation, their fatalism. Generally, they feel that few things make a difference; that environmental context dominates their effectiveness; that the future is uncontrollable; and that they are unable to influence things for the better. This mindset strangles organisational effectiveness: it leads to poor performance in companies and, in the public sector, it undermines the achievement of the purpose to enhance and equalise life-chances.

A key to tackling this mindset is the encouragement of a trustworthy and innovative climate at work. The box below shows a simple checklist for promoting trust in organisations.

To earn trust

- Actively listen to others.
- Tell the truth.
- Be open.
- Share information.
- Avoid petty disputes.
- Don't personalise.
- Compromise, collaborate.
- Keep conflict functional.
- Always look for win–wins.
- Allow people to save face.

Innovation is the source of enhanced operational effectiveness in local government as elsewhere. In large organisations, it needs nurturing and encouragement. But we know that the majority of innovations do not lead to progress. In fact, we only achieve progress through a proper understanding of our errors. But, in too many Councils, error has few friends. The adversarial nature of politics at the local and national level too often leads to a situation where mistakes are penalised. Local politicians need to appreciate the hard truth that, if you don't want to get anything wrong, don't expect to do anything new. And it is the role of organisational leadership to ensure that a sophisticated six-syllable word called 'accountability' is not swiftly and easily compressed into a shorter and cruder word – 'blame'.

The essence of progressive organisations is their ability to learn critically from their mistakes and their errors. Thus, the public sector needs a better understanding of the nature of risk taking (what sort of risks should public servants be encouraged to take with the public's money and what should they not?). Yes, there are 'first mover disadvantages' in the public sector just as there are in the private sector, but it is possible to encourage innovation while minimising risk to the public.

'We are all good people trapped in a bad system'

This is the cry of the postmodern worker. Why is it that we have fine intentions, carefully crafted strategies, properly resourced project plans, adequately trained customer service staff and, yet, we still seem to fail our citizens and our customers? This apparent truth leads many in local government to consider that ineffectiveness must arise from some systemic failure beyond our control or some otherwise intrinsic feature of public service provision. But that's not so. Some private sector companies fail altogether and a great deal more fail their customers. The fact that public institutions can't fail should not mean that they can fail even more of their customers than their private sector counterparts.

Councils are public institutions and as such have a legal and constitutional status, but they are socially constructed. It's the people in them that make them work or fail. It's no good blaming the construct when the essence of organisation is something that we have built ourselves. And, so, the contention here is that if local government is ineffective it's our own feckless fatalism or our own reckless certainties that are at fault. If things are not going well, there is no one to blame but ourselves. We socially construct the system that we then claim traps us from being effective.

So how can good people escape the trap? First, by being open and honest about the failings and deficiencies in the present state of local government. As has been noted elsewhere in this paper (but which bears repetition), disclosing our dissatisfaction with the present is the prerequisite for progressive change. Putting the past behind you is an important first step in your forward journey.

A thorough managerial approach to delivering progressive change in local government contains four interconnected strands.

9 FOUR STRANDS IN LEADING PROGRESSIVE MANAGERIAL CHANGE

When appraising a Council's performance, it is right to focus on the quality of its management but it is more apposite to focus on the quality of its managers' efforts. In short, we should not have an overly *ad hominem* approach to local government. Councils don't fail because they have weak people, they fail because their people do things weakly. Modern Councils need to have managerial and employee strategies that have four main strands:

- well-designed internal accountabilities for effective performance

- managerial competencies to ensure personal capability

- organisational culture, systems and processes to ensure organisational capability

- a focus on personal efficacy to ensure personal confidence and ambition.

Strand 1: organisational design

The internal accountabilities within a Council are traditionally organised through varied professional prisms and exemplified in the 'organogram' that shows how teams are brigaded into divisions, departments, directorates and ultimately into the whole organisation. How responsibilities are designed is as important to focusing operational service delivery as it is to understanding the corporate management arrangements of the authority. But it is the latter that gains the most attention. In a sense, a new 'boxology' has been created where Chief Executives fashion new designs to refocus the most senior managerial attention within their organisations. The term that is used most in this context is 'structure': an odd term in that what are actually meant are the lines of managerial accountabilities within the Council.

Those responsible for redesigning a Council's management arrangements need to take full account of the performance requirements of the organisation, its legal competencies and its budget availability, the need for complementarity at the most senior level, and the organisation's succession needs. Redesigning the accountability of management within organisations is not, contrary to the views of many, a fad of newly appointed Chief Executives. The need to revise organisational design stems from the:

- increasing complexity of coordinating a diverse but interdependent organisation to deliver modern services to citizens

- increasing need to work effectively across boundaries, building investment and service partnerships with both private sector partners and other public agencies

- developing 'externalisation' of some functions (housing etc.) and new funding mechanisms, which may lead to massive changes to the scale and balance of resources within the organisation.

Consequently, senior managers in Councils are increasingly being required to provide leadership capacity and performance capability across the whole organisation; hence, the new focus on the role of the 'top teams' in local government. Management teams at the top differ from other managerial teams because of their special responsibilities and unique leadership role. To achieve their objectives, they need to be organised for:

- discipline: integrating executive leadership across the organisation to energise initiative and performance

- alignment: orchestrating the behaviour and decisions of people throughout the organisation

- balance: reflecting the complexity of the demands on the organisation with a flexibility of managerial skills, thereby optimising leadership capacity and performance.

The role of the senior executives in local government is not only to manage functions but also to harness the corporate synergy that flows from the management of distinct functions in a combined fashion. If Councils are to continue as multi-purpose bodies, they need to better link their purposes together to achieve community benefits. And this can only be achieved if councillors conduct their politics corporately and managers reflect and reinforce this local corporate political approach.

Large organisations always have two powerful forces acting against the efforts of those responsible for designing corporate responses to external challenges. The first force is the inevitable Balkanising tendency of middle managers. The second is the standardising tendency of the technocrats. But local government displays more inertia than other comparable organisations because it has a powerful third force – the professionalised experts. Hence, it is no good modernising political governance arrangements while leaving the traditional guild professional structure of local government intact. Functions need to be grouped in significant blocks so as to force service synergies (over professional boundaries and rigidities). Departmentalism is the main barrier to developing corporate responses to local social problems. Organisational design that is service focused is essential.

Furthermore, the design of management accountabilities is linked to organisational service strategies. The connection between strategic plan and operational delivery is so often where things fail. Often failure arrives because those who devised the strategy (to solve the problem or to heighten performance) are too involved in developing the strategy further. Over-elaborated strategies owned by fewer and fewer people will always fare worse against simple strategies that are widely owned. The direction that needs to be followed (as well as that which is to be avoided) is set out in Figure 6.

Figure 6 Devising a successful strategy

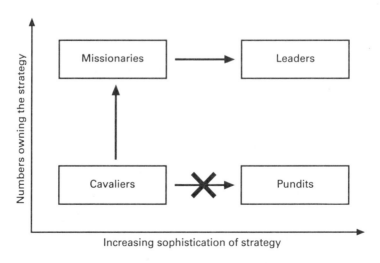

Strand 2: managerial and organisational competencies

Lower than expected organisational performance can stem either from incapability, or from incompetence or low motivation and/ or commitment. Knowing the difference between the two is central to effective leadership. Leaders of teams and organisations must therefore ensure that the people they manage have the capabilities and competence to perform successfully. Creating the conditions for a capable and competent organisation is crucial for success. Managers need to be competent for the coming age as well as capable of meeting today's demands. This means that Councils need a refreshed 'suite of competencies' for their managers. Too few Councils have competency-based staff profiles and training and development schemes. What is more, these competencies are likely to be common across the public sector agencies within localities. In the box below is a modular suite of competencies for the current age that is being used by one Council. In this example, managers are advised for each competence what behaviour accords with the respective competencies and what behaviour does not.

But competencies alone are not enough: they provide a platform for personal capability. What is also needed is organisational capability. Traditionally, organisational capability has been best understood by reference to an organisation's assets and resources (its offices, its staff or its money), or by its distinctiveness, its uniqueness or its special strengths (such as project management, financial controls or marketing). And, in many ways, this remains the case.

A disciplined approach to budget management, legal competence, performance target setting, resource deployment and operational delivery is central to our understanding of an organisation's capabilities. And these disciplines are essential.

Model competencies

Continuous improvement

- Inspirational leadership
- Thinking broadly
- Focus on change

Working together

- Working in partnership
- Influencing
- Communication

Tackling service issues

- Problem solving
- Decision making

Delivering services

- Planning and implementation
- Customer focus
- Self-management
- Achieving results

When in place, they become the fundamentals of the organisation. If the disciplines of performance management, budgetary control and operational quality management are in place, Councils should not fail. But, with only these, they still may not succeed.

Strand 3: progressive organisational culture

It is now widely accepted that an organisation adds value to individuals through the way that knowledge is shared, both formally and informally, and through its wider cultural climate. In the present age, it is exceptionally difficult for anyone's knowledge to stay current. And this problem is heightened in local government given the array of 'expert' professionals who need continually to refresh their knowledge (social work, civil engineering, planning, accountancy, legal and so on). So the present added advantage to individuals of working in an organisation is that it helps you to stay current. But does it?

Professional knowledge workers are the very essence of local government and their effectiveness is, in large part, offered by discretion to their Council. Establishing a sound basis for sharing knowledge within an organisation is becoming one of the best means of harnessing the discretionary effort of these knowledge workers. Thus, political and managerial leaders in local government need to examine how they can shape their organisations' knowledge-sharing capability as well as attract and retain people, before they consider how to mobilise the best from the people they have.

The second key feature for discussion here is the cultural climate within an organisation. The culture of an organisation is evident to those within it, to its customers and to visitors. Charles Handy captures this point when he comments:

> Organisations have a feel about them, a feel which the visitor picks up as soon as he or she enters the building or, often, merely encounters one of the people who work there. There is an abundance of what can best be called the 'E' factors, when 'E' stands for energy, enthusiasm, effort, excitement, excellence and so on. More than that the talk is about 'we' not 'I', and there is a sense that the organisation is on a crusade, not just to make money, but something grander, something worthy of one's commitment, skills and time.
>
> (Handy, 1997)

As ever, Handy expresses the essence of success. Successful organisations have not only a culture of disciplined planning and achievement, but also reservoirs of positive energy. They are 'communities of practice' that help their members drive strategy, start new lines of business, solve problems more quickly, transfer best practice and develop their skills and talent. And the leaders in these organisations are keenly focused on how best they can release the positive energy within their staff.

Recent research among local authority staff has shown that a minority (about one-quarter) consider that change is well managed in their Councils, with poor communication and ineffective management feedback being the main cause of staff dissatisfaction. Councils need to recognise that staff communication, development and engagement is central to improving performance. Moreover, it is the case that operational front-line staff need at least as much development and attention as professional and strategic staff if Council services are genuinely to improve.

But today's workers don't just want to work in a place with 'buzz'; they also want to work in a place that enables them to build their own sense of belonging. For, at a time when the pace of everyday life combines with fractures in traditional families, people seem to be seeking a sense of attachment and belonging in community. And, despite the increasingly temporary nature of work, it offers as good a prospect for developing a sense of belonging as elsewhere. Indeed, local government is the only place where the vocational community and the locational community coincide; hence the immense opportunity to tap the added sense of attachment and commitment that this inevitably gives to local government staff.

Local government managers also need to see how their various service areas and the staff they manage connect with the organisation's wider purposes. At bottom, this capacity 'to connect' individual staff to some wider (possibly some, dare the term be used, nobler) purpose is central to managers' role as leaders. They need to ground their service purpose in the Council's broader mission.

Local government managers also need to have an orientation that is responsible, respectful, rational and results oriented – one that exercises power and authority in a responsible manner; one that is respectful of the individuality of those who are managed; one that explains the reasons for the direction of the service; and one that is results focused. They need to learn how to build trustworthiness into the work practice in their organisations.

For managers to embrace this ethic, they need to be both self-aware and self-confident. Personal competence and organisational capability create the conditions for success. They do not create success. Success stems when capable people in capable organisations believe they can effect change and cause it to happen. This is the key ingredient of success. Competent people in capable organisations focused on doing the right thing can, unfortunately, still fail to succeed. More likely, they will perform moderately well. But is it well enough?

Strand 4: personal and organisational efficacy

"Why should I use my best efforts and talents to improve the Council's performance and, even if I did put all my energies and expertise at the Council's disposal, my guess is that it wouldn't make any difference anyway."

This is the key double-barrelled question in every worker's head. If those with political and managerial leadership responsibility in local government can come close to answering or resolving this key question, considerable progress can be made in enhancing organisational effectiveness.

Councils, like all large organisations, are composed of people who can produce more common good by their collective efforts than they are able to as individuals acting alone. However, two considerations may act to inhibit them. First, they may rationally decide to 'free-ride' on the efforts of others; and, second, they may feel that they cannot themselves cause change anyway. Indeed, these two considerations are interrelated. For, if I consider that my efforts cannot cause the change the organisation desires, I am more inclined to free-ride on the efforts of others. Unchecked, this mindset can strangle organisational effectiveness.

For, while people may have a common interest in producing collective benefits, they may have no common interest in paying the cost of providing that collective good. They need to be convinced that their efforts are making a difference to the collective efforts produced without them. Moreover, they would be more likely to contribute their efforts if they believed that they would produce not only collective benefits but also personal benefits to them that they would not obtain by 'free-riding'. This is, therefore, one of the central tasks of organisational leadership: to galvanise people's individual contributions into a broader collective effort. It applies in schools, in service areas and in Councils overall.

Leadership is not simply a question of releasing ability and ambition. Ability and ambition alone are, unfortunately, not enough. Leaders help people raise their effectiveness, not just their sights. And, to be personally effective, people need knowledge of their own abilities and a sense that they can cause change. A belief in one's capability to cause change is crucial. It is the basis of self-efficacy.

It starts with an internalised view of external events and a positive assessment of one's ability to control or influence these events. It is more than the adoption of a positive optimistic mindset (which, contrary to popular misconception, can be acquired). Indeed, it has been appreciated for some 30 years that behaviour is influenced by anticipated outcomes. But outcomes arise from actions. How one behaves largely determines the outcomes one experiences. In this way, performance is causally prior to outcomes. People do not judge that they will drown if they jump into deep water and then infer that they might be poor swimmers. Rather, people who judge themselves to be poor swimmers will visualise themselves drowning if they jump into deep water.

Thus, the final strand in building a progressive managerial approach involves developing employees' sense of self-efficacy. This is a judgement of one's ability to organise and execute given types of performance. The concept of self-efficacy is vitally important to organisational effectiveness. The relationship between individuals and their environment is reciprocally deterministic, not independent: they create each other. People may use their internal concept of their own efficacy to adapt to their environment or to change it. Importantly, people's efficacy is not a fixed capability (like their personalities) but rather it is generative. People who doubt their capabilities in particular areas shy away from difficult tasks in these domains, while people who have strong beliefs in their capabilities approach difficult tasks as challenges to be mastered rather than as threats to be avoided. So, a key task for leaders of organisations is to help people build and develop their own sense of self-efficacy.

When people in an organisation have a shared belief in their joint capability to organise and execute the course of action necessary to achieve desired levels of attainment, they have collective efficacy. And it is this that organisations seek. Successful organisations understand the complexity of what they face but they do not give in to the forces of fatalism. Instead, they appraise their capabilities and affirm their belief that they can achieve their goals through collective action. Leaders in those organisations know that disciplined execution is necessary but they also know that those doing the execution are people with emotions, ambitions and fears.

Our mood biases our attention and affects how events are interpreted. A prevailing positive mood in an organisation promotes success, while a despondent mood leads people to underestimate their capability to perform. Effective leaders therefore actively seek to create a positive mood or climate in their organisations. Positive moods are conducive to risk taking, creativity, innovation and a sense of well-being throughout the organisation.

Negative moods produce a climate dominated by a fear of failure. This drives people to avoid commitment. And people who avoid commitment will not give their best or their all. Hence, if accountability in Councils operates entirely within a partisan framework and where scrutiny is characterised by negative fault finding, the organisational culture will be one of detachment and avoidance. Effective leaders use 'soft skills' to produce hard results. They use intangibles and symbols (such as staff recognition and valuing staff events) to create a positive mood in their organisations.

Organisational cultures have powerful consequences on behaviour. There are for all of us twice as many negative emotions (fear, grief, anxiety, embarrassment, shame, guilt and so on) as positive ones and, in consequence, losses are felt more keenly than gains. This psychological asymmetry results in people making bigger commitments to avoid sure losses than to obtain sure gains. And, so, the fear of failure always lives with us in constant tension with our internal drive for recognition and success. Given that the nature of our psychological condition is such, it is perhaps best to adopt the stance suggested in the song by Johnny Mercer:

"Accentuate the positive,
Eliminate the negative,
Latch on to the affirmative,
Don't mess with Mister in-between"
(Ac-cent-tchu-ate the positive)

The playwright, Alan Bennett, illustrates this point with his usual acute observation. He suggests (with a little exaggeration to make the point) that it is temperament and self-esteem rather than a good education that best enables people to succeed. Moreover, he suggests that the biggest barrier to social advancement in England is not the entrenched social class system but the fear of embarrassment that envelopes the English.

Whatever the precise cultural traits involved in English local government, the key point is that an organisation with well-designed internal accountabilities, well-developed approaches to fostering competencies among its employees and a 'can do' entrepreneurial culture will still fail if its people do not believe that they can cause the progressive change the organisation desires.

This is a vital lesson for – among others – the leadership in schools, because the barriers to educational success are as much in the social norms of the school as they are in the social background of the pupils. Perhaps, above all, a progression and achievement orientation within a school stems from the climate or ethos of the school created by teachers who exude a sense of efficacy and ambition for their pupils. And, if pupils' parents and peers share this sense of efficacy, they can be even more effective.

In any collective endeavour, the role of leadership is to enhance people's shared belief in their conjoint capability to organise and execute the course of action required to achieve their shared aims and objectives. But this is extraordinarily difficult to achieve, as there are very significant dilemmas to people in deciding whether or not to participate in collective action of any sort.

But collective success brings benefits to the participants as individuals. Participants in collective endeavours are usually united in a cohesive community that touches many aspects of their lives. And a strong sense of camaraderie can provide sustaining interpersonal rewards at times when the tangible benefit of social change may be long in coming.

However, many people shy away from collective action not because they calculate that they can gain the benefits without the costs of participation but because they seriously doubt the group's efficacy in securing any benefits at all. It is therefore crucial that organisational leaders can demonstrate precisely how organisational capability can bolster the added efforts of individuals. As was shown above, fashioning a critical mass of activists around progressive change is more likely to succeed than requiring the immediate participation of everyone.

Successful leaders are not just at 'the top' of the organisation. Leadership skills need to exist throughout organisations for them to be successful. Successful leaders seem to combine an excitement towards the organisation's goals with humility towards the people they lead. Leaders need to exude vitality, dynamism and positive energy to encourage a positive mood to deliver success and to maintain a momentum for progressive change. They need to ensure that belief in progressive change is rooted in a realistic understanding of the current complexities but finally, as ever, they must also convey that 'the way things presently are' is simply not good enough for the community of people we are here to serve.

10 CONCLUSION: A TEN-POINT BLUEPRINT

Local government is currently immersed in heated debates about models of governance and approaches to service delivery. These heated debates leave the public cold. They just want Councils to be relevant to their lives, provide services of quality and excellence and, where appropriate, help them swim safely in the turbulence of the current age.

English local government faces considerable changes. But citizens need more than a reorganised local politics and much more than increasingly efficient models for service delivery. In this fast developing globalising era, there are signs that there is a real 'retreat to locality': to what is closest. Leadership at the local government level involves building a sense of place and belonging. Local leadership also involves building a sense of community and common purpose. In the current age, a renewed sense of place and locality is a good step, but it is not enough. Locality is more than geography, topography and landscape. Locality is the theatre of economic, social and political relations: a place for conflict and drama as well as culture and contentment.

Thus, local government's leaders need to develop both a new spirit of community (a new localism) and a new public spirit for community (a new civicism). Building common cause locally across organisations and sectors requires leadership of the highest order able to shape an *esprit de corps* beyond organisational boundaries. But it is not possible for local government to lead across sectors and boundaries if they are unable to lead their own organisations effectively.

The most successful organisations in both private and public sectors have the dual characteristics of 'clouds' and 'clocks'. Clouds give expression to the organisation's ideals and ideas. They inspire people. They are emergent, inchoate, have reservoirs of positive energy, and they lack rigid internal boundaries. Clocks by contrast are orderly, precise and disciplined. Their activities are regular and routine. If leaders are able to keep this duality (of clouds and clocks) dynamic and real within their organisations, they are likely to create the conditions for a successful enterprise.

Local government currently faces enormous challenges. Some have been set formally by the Government but far more are set everyday by citizens. Jack Welch of General Electric says that, in today's world, job security is provided not by companies but only by customers. In local government, security comes not from the Government but from local citizens.

The wisdom of experience is that 'the intractable problems of the moment' melt away with time. The impossibilities of cabinet and scrutiny government, the contradictions of managerial and political executives, and the inexplicable demise of local democratic traditions will each pass into a different phase. What is now leading edge will become passé in months, conventional within years and will create its own problems within a decade. What appears insoluble now, according to Jung, can only be outgrown:

> All the greatest and most important problems in life are fundamentally insoluble … They can never be solved but only outgrown. This 'outgrowing' proves on further investigation to require a new level of consciousness. Some further or wider interest appears on the horizon and through this broadening of outlook the insoluble problem loses its urgency.
>
> (quoted in Mulgan, 1998)

The problems of local government are not so great that a new level of consciousness is required. But a progressive optimism of spirit is called for among those with leadership positions. An optimistic organisation has habits of learning that encourage its staff to particularise failure or misfortune as opportunities for learning and to acquire habits of thinking that focus on how they can be more successful in the future.

This essay argues that local Councils need a disciplined approach to designing and delivering services as well as a spirit to succeed as community leaders. To do this, effective political leadership needs to be in tandem with effective managerial leadership. Both need to appreciate how best to release energy and inspire progressive change within their organisation and across their community. There are no 'magic potions' for leading progressive change but the following ten-point plan presents a blueprint of sorts.

First, the Government needs to recognise that even when extrinsic incentives for local government are both significant and coordinated – as with the local public service agreements (PSAs), or those proposed in *Towards a New Localism* – they still do not guarantee that Councils will all change in the same intended direction.

Second, it is vital that the political and managerial leadership in Councils pays adequate attention to the fundamentals of service delivery and budget management. The first step of reputation management is getting the fundamentals (refuse collection, protecting children at risk, etc.) absolutely right and maintaining financial control. Combining quality management approaches with rigorous budgetary planning and controls is the bedrock of disciplined operational excellence.

Third, all Council services need to be continually appraised for their relevance to the (emerging) needs of service users, and designed and delivered to provide real value to users regardless of any vested municipalist or contracted interests. Best value ought not to become a new elaborate process management regime but should be focused tightly on ensuring, first, relevance; and, second, significant productivity improvements in all local public services.

Fourth, Councils need to exploit the opportunities of e-business and deliver services on an expanded variety of delivery channels and over an expanded time horizon (while attempting to reduce the cost base of these channels). The agenda of web-enabled government will not simply alter the cost base for public services but will also move the public sector more towards an empowering and self-service approach. Grasping this agenda for service delivery and improved connection with citizens will be central to local government retaining its relevance over the medium term.

Fifth, Councils need to realise that development at the local level is more than site assembly and business partnerships; it is intimately connected at the local level with the expansion of civil freedoms and progressive forms of civic engagement. And, if Councils are to increase their democratic legitimacy, they need to adopt more imaginative and inclusive approaches to engaging with citizens and civil society.

Sixth, at the local level, the quality of political leadership is crucial to producing an organisational climate that is creative, innovative and conducive to progressive change. Radical change is required. The numbers and roles of councillors need examination (or clearer separation is required between smaller directly elected political executives and larger community councils). And urgent consideration is merited towards adopting a fairer system of election locally. Political parties at the local level need to develop activism among local citizens as well as in their party. And local political leadership ought not to be left to chance but needs to be an active feature in Government, LGA and IDEA programmes.

Seventh, Councils need to design managerial accountabilities within their organisations so as to aid service effectiveness and corporate responsiveness. The professional guild structure that typifies tradition in local government needs to be replaced by a more outward-facing organisational design. Moreover, the links and accountabilities between political and managerial executives need very careful working through to avoid overlapping and confused responsibilities or improper hybridity in decision making.

Eighth, Councils need to develop the competencies of all their staff and ensure their organisations have aligned all available resources to guarantee their collective capability as well as a culture that encourages entrepreneurship and success. Excellence in operational management stems from excellence in people management and in people development. Councils need to develop 'deep leadership' throughout their staff rather than focus leadership at 'the top' of the management structure.

Ninth, Councils need actively to manage information and knowledge for their critical use by staff, councillors and citizens. The prolific expansion of knowledge and information is bewildering to everyone. The information resources of Councils should be used to help people navigate their own way through the blizzards of the information age.

Tenth, Councils need to enhance the internal sense of efficacy of their staff and councillors, for, unless they have the belief that together they can cause progressive change and the ambition to make it happen, all the other ingredients could result in unrealised hopes.

For Councils to succeed in the current age, they need inspired leadership that is ethical and directional. The ethical base stems from a concern with furthering the 'public interest' locally. And the direction stems from the desire to build a positive sense of place and to improve the quality of life and life-chances of those living locally. Councils need political and managerial leaders who are fired by excitement and energy when it is directed towards organisational goals but characterised by humility when it is focused on people. Leadership of this nature will concentrate on win–wins with local partners for common cause and the public good.

Esprit de corps

The essence of this essay is that locality matters most to most people. That healthy local government is crucial to healthy local communities. That the localities that will succeed in the modern world will have, among many other positive features, an outgoing self-confidence. And, finally, that the role of local government is to create the conditions for success locally and to generate self-confidence – amongst councillors, staff and throughout local civic society.

Increased citizen involvement is central to raising service quality and to improving local democracy. But Councils need to do more than simply involve people. They also need to re-kindle a sense of spirit in their communities. And not just any spirit but a progressive and civic-minded spirit that is pluralist and raises the public interest over private and vested interests. Furthermore, Councils have ample resources and opportunities to achieve this objective. They also need to recognise the power of symbolically inclusive local civic events and incidents that help to create the basis for important and affirming collective memories in communities. These events can provide a tangible sense of shared heritage in a locality as well as creating a common language, idiom and sense of identity.

Spirited communities need spirited Councils. And spirited Councils are built by the people in them; not according to a plan drawn up in Whitehall. They are composed of people who are critical and enquiring as well as being future oriented and community minded. These Councils are composed of inspiring politicians in touch with local civil society. And they encourage their organisations to be composed of managers and employees who are civic entrepreneurs, seeking opportunities and mobilising public resources for social benefit.

If Councils are to succeed, they need inspired leadership that is ethical and directional. They need leadership that is fired by excitement and energy when it is directed towards organisational goals but characterised by humility when it is focused on people. Leadership of this nature will focus on win–wins with local partners for common cause and the public good.

Councils need to develop a sense of *esprit de corps* amongst their politicians, managers and employees. This spirit of common cause needs to be infectious across the organisation's boundaries to embrace public and private partners as well as community organisations – an *esprit de corps* not just for its own sake, but to build a distinctive and affirming sense of place and locality. Progressive change in local government cannot be willed into action by central government. External incentives help but there is no substitute for local politicians, community leaders and Council officers creating progressive change for social purpose from the apparently hopeless inertia in which they find themselves. Leadership, both political and managerial, is needed not to invoke progressive change but to generate it.

REFERENCES AND FURTHER READING

1 Introduction

Castells, M. (1997) *The Network Society*. Blackwell
Freidman, T. (2000) *The Lexus and the Olive Tree*. HarperCollins
Giddens, A. (1999) *Runaway World*. Profile
Hutton, W. and Giddens, A. (eds) (2000) *On the Edge*. Jonathan Cape
Mazarr, M. (1999) *Global Trends 2005*. Macmillan
Norris, P. (1999) *Critical Citizens*. Oxford University Press
Pharr, S. and Putnam, R. (eds) (2000) *Disaffected Democracies*. Princeton

2 The character of change and progress

Berlin, I. (1990) *The Crooked Timber of Humanity*. Princeton
Bronk, A. (1998) *Progress and the Invisible Hand*. Warner Books
Goss, S. and Leadbetter, C. (1998) *Civic Entrepreneurship*. Demos
Gould, S. (1996) *Life's Grandeur*. Jonathan Cape
Porter, R. (2000) *Enlightenment*. Allen Lane
Sagan, C. (1997) *Demon-haunted World*. Headline
Williams, R. (1976) *Keywords*. Fontana

3 The changing character of leadership

Cabinet Office (2000a) *People's Panel Fifth Wave Results*. HMSO
De Pree, M. (1989) *Leadership is an Art*. Arrow
Drucker, P. (1996) *The Leader of the Future*. Jossey-Bass
Gardner, H. (1997) *Leading Minds*. Basic Books
Goleman, D. (2000) 'Leadership that gets results', *Harvard Business Review*,
    March–April, pp. 78–90

Kouzes, J. and Posner, B. (1993) *Credibility*. Jossey-Bass
Kouzes, J. and Posner, B. (1995) *The Leadership Challenge*. Jossey-Bass
Kouzes, J. and Posner, B. (1999) *Encouraging the Heart*. Jossey-Bass

4 The Government's agenda for change

Bryson, J. and Crosby, B. (1992) *Leadership for the Common Good*. Jossey-Bass
Cabinet Office (1999) *Modernising Government*. HMSO
Cabinet Office (2000a) *Peoples Panel Fifth Wave Results*. HMSO
Cabinet Office (2000b) *Reaching Out*. Performance & Innovation Unit, HMSO
Filkin, G. *et al.* (2000) *Towards a New Localism*. NLGN
Kickert, W. *et al.* (1997) *Managing Complex Networks*. Sage
Perri 6 *et al.* (1999) *Governing in the Round*. Demos
Rhodes, R. (2000) *The Governance Narrative*. Public Management & Policy Association

5 Delivering greater productivity

Deming, W. (1996) *New Economics*. Harvard University Press
Filkin, G. *et al.* (2000) *Towards a New Localism*. NLGN
Kaplan, R. and Norton, D. (1996) *The Balanced Scorecard*. Harvard Business School Press
Kelly, R.M. (ed.) (1988) *Promoting Productivity in the Public Sector*. Macmillan
Lane, J.-E. (2000) *New Public Management*. Routledge
Murphy, B. (2000) *The Local Government Improvement Programme: a Year in Focus*. IDEA
Olve, N.-G. *et al.* (2000) *Performance Drivers*. Wiley
Productivity Services Panel (2000) *Meeting the Challenge*. HM Treasury

6 Progressive change in service delivery

Performance & Innovation Unit (2000) *Electronic Government Services for the 21st Century*. HMSO
Cabinet Office (2000a) *E-government*. HMSO
Cabinet Office (2000b) *Citizens 1st*. HMSO
National Audit Office (2000) *Supporting Innovation*. National Audit Office
Newman, J. *et al.* (2000) *Innovation and Best Practice in Local Government*. DETR

7 Progressive change in local politics and governance

Bauman, Z. (2001) *Community*. Polity

Crick, B. (2000) *Essays on Citizenship*. Continuum

Dahl, R. (1998) *On Democracy*. Yale

Dunleavy, P. and Margetts, H. (1999) *Proportional Representation and Local Government*. JRF

Elser, J. (ed.) (1998) *Deliberative Democracy*. Cambridge

Hammond, J. *et al*. (1999) *Smart Choices*. Harvard Business School Press

Hetherington, P. (2000) *Back to the Future*. Local Government Association

Kirkham, A. *et al*. (2000) *Active Democracy*. JRF Charitable Trust

Leach, S. and Game, C. (2000) *Hung Authorities, Elected Mayors and Cabinet Government*. JRF

Parston, G. and Cowe, I. (1998) *Making the Connections*. Public Management Foundation

Putnam, R. (2000) *Bowling Alone*. Simon & Schuster

Przeworski, A. *et al*. (eds) (1999) *Democracy, Accountability and Representation*. Cambridge University Press

Rudat, K. (2000) *2020 Public Visions for Local Governance*. NLGN

Sen, A. (1999) *Development as Freedom*. Anchor

Sullivan, D. (2000) 'Proportional presentation', *Local Government Chronicle*, 26 July

Wright, C. (2000) *A Community Manifesto*. Earthscan

8 Progressive change in management and organisation

Clarke, T. and Clegg, S. (2000) *Changing Paradigms*. Harper Collins Business

Evans, P. and Wurster, T. (2000) *Blown to Bits*. Harvard Business School Press

Filkin, G. *et al*. (2000) *Towards a New Localism*. NLGN

Katzenbach, J. (1998) *Teams at the Top*. Harvard Business School Press

Mintzberg, H. (1993) *Structure in Fives*. Prentice Hall

Mintzberg, H. *et al*. (1998) *Strategy Safari*. Prentice Hall

Nadler, D. *et al*. (1998) *Executive Teams*. Jossey-Bass

Nalbandian, J. (1994) 'The reflections of a "pracademic" on the logic of politics and administration', *Public Administration Review*, Vol. 54, No. 6, November–December, pp. 531–6

Patler, L. (1999) *Tilt!* Capstone

Taffinder, P. (1999) *Big Change*. Wiley

9 Four strands of progressive management

Bandura, A. (1997) *Self-efficacy*. Freeman

Carnevale, D. (1999) *Trustworthy Government*. Jossey-Bass

Chowdury, S. (ed.) (2000) *Management 21C*. FT-Prentice Hall

Fineman, S. (ed.) (2000) *Emotion in Organisations*. 2nd edition. Sage

Handy, C. (1997) *The Hungry Spirit*. Arrow

Irwin, F. (1971) *Intentional Behaviour*. Lippincott

London Borough of Lewisham (2000) *The Lewisham Manager*. London Borough of Lewisham

MORI (2000) 'Research among local authority staff' [http://www.mori.co.uk]

Olson, M. (1971) *The Logic of Collective Action*. Harvard University Press

Seligman, M. (1998) *Learned Optimism*. Pocket Books

Sennett, R. (1998) *The Corrosion of Character*. Norton

Tice, L. (1999) *Self-efficacy*. The Pacific Institute – Seattle

10 Conclusion: a ten-point blueprint

Filkin, G. *et al.* (2000) *Towards a New Localism*. NLGN

Hesselbein, F. et al. (eds) (1998) *The Community of the Future*. Jossey-Bass

Mulgan, G. (1998) 'Timeless values', in I. Christie and L. Nash (eds) *The Good Life*. Demos

Owen, H. (2000) *The Power of Spirit*. Berrett Koehler

Purdy, J. (2000) *For Common Things*. Vintage

Scott, M. (2000) *Reinspiring the Corporation*. Wiley

Spitzer, R. (2000) *The Spirit of Leadership*. Executive Excellence

Wenger, E. and Snyder, W. (2000) 'Communities of practice', *Harvard Business Review*, January–February, pp. 139–45